ULTIMATE GUIDE TO PERSONAL FREEDOM

—— AND ——

FULFILLMENT

1000

TIMELESS QUOTES & WISDOM KEYS ON LIVING WELL

EDITOR: FRANCIS E.U.

Published by KHARIS PUBLISHING, an imprint of
KHARIS MEDIA LLC.

Copyright © 2024 Francis E. U.

ISBN-13: 978-1-63746-240-9

ISBN-10: 1-63746-240-9

Library of Congress Control Number: 2024931702

All KHARIS PUBLISHING products are available at
special quantity discounts for bulk purchase for sales
promotions, premiums, fund-raising, and educational
needs. For details, contact:

Kharis Media LLC
Tel: 1-630-909-3405
support@kharispublishing.com
www.kharispublishing.com

Contents

Introduction:

Who and what motivate you?

Throughout our lives, we get advice, guidance, direction and criticism from others, whether we ask for it, deserve it, need it, or not. Each of us can easily recall and recite familiar or famous words we've memorized to keep us moving forward, to keep us from giving up, and even to keep us from gloating. Whether it's our careers, our relationships, our beliefs, our pleasures and our pains, somebody, somewhere, had something to share, say and pray. Motivational quotes or affirmations are meant to inspire us, as well as confirm we're on track to reach our goals, but they also are meant to stop us in our tracks, examine our rhymes and reasons, and even laugh at ourselves.

Perhaps you have a favorite quote, a "tried and true" phrase that you call to mind when you need to;

maybe you have your favorite saying on a sticky note tacked up above your desk. Perhaps that favorite quote is among the 1,000 quotes in this book. Even if your favorite quote is here, there are 999 more for you to read and consider.; even if you find you already know 999 of these quotes, there will be one more for you to learn and take to heart. Thumb through these pages, find words that affirm, inspire, intrigue, and humble you, along with some well-chosen quotes to tickle your funny bone.

Here are the first 30 wisdom keys to help you on your journey to becoming the best version of yourself in all the paths, mazes, dangerous curves, and delightful pathways you may find beneath your feet... After all, keeping your feet on the ground and your head in the clouds is a fine way to live. Remember, Henry Ford said: "Whether you think you can, or you think you can't, you're correct."

30 Wisdom Keys to Inspire you to Aspire

1. The great use of life is to spend it for something that will outlast it. — William James

2. Be teachable. You are not always right. — Unknown

3. Life is not about how fast you run or how high you climb, but how well you bounce. — Vivian Komori

4. Hope is like a road in the country; there was never a road but when many people walk on it, the road comes into existence. — Lin Yutang

5. Almost everything will work if you unplug it for a few minutes, including you. — Anne Lamont

6. How wonderful it is that nobody need wait a single moment before starting to improve the world. — Anne Frank

7. You have a greater potential than anyone who has ever lived before you! But you'll never "make it" by sitting on your duff and telling the world how great you're going to be, starting tomorrow. — Og Mandingo

8. Stop waiting for the right time. Time isn't waiting for you. — Unknown

9. The biggest adventure you can ever take is to live the life of your dreams. — Oprah Winfrey

10. It always seems impossible until it's done. — Nelson Mandela

11. The way to get started is to quit talking and begin doing. — Walt Disney

12. Making mistakes is better than faking perfection. — Esther Dyson

13. The greater danger for most of us lies not in setting our aim too high and falling short, but in setting our aim too low and achieving our mark. — Michelangelo

14. If only the sun-drenched celebrities are being noticed and worshipped, then our children are going to have a tough time seeing value in the shadows, where the thinkers, probers, and scientists are keeping society together. — Rita Dove

15. Nobody is coming to save you. Get up and be your own hero. — Kevin Mangelschots

16. If you hear a voice within you saying, "You are not a painter," then by all means paint, boy, and that voice will be silenced, but only by working. — Vincent van Gogh

17. Life is meant to be lived, and curiosity must be kept alive. One must never, for whatever reason, turn his back on life. — Eleanor Roosevelt

18. Your comfort zone will destroy your dreams. — Unknown

19. Stop calling it a dream and start calling it a plan. — The Purpose Exchange

20. If you can build a muscle, you can build a mindset. — Paul Corke

21. A champion is someone who gets up when he can't. — Jack Dempsey

22. If you control your thoughts, you control your life.— Unknown

23. Your time is your most precious asset. Don't waste it. — Mel Robbins

24. Your comfort zone is killing your potential. — A. Hafidh

25. Just because it's not what you were expecting, doesn't mean it's not everything you need right now. — Paulo Coelho

26. Chase your passion, not your pension. — Denis Waitley

27. Do not let making a living prevent you from making a life. — John Wooden

28. The question isn't who is going to let me; it's who is going to stop me. — Ayn Rand

29. The saddest aspect of life right now is that science gathers knowledge faster than society gathers wisdom. — Isaac Asimov

30. The sun will rise and set regardless. What we choose to do with the light while it's here is up to us. Journey wisely. — Alexandra Elle

Chapter One

Self-knowledge
and Self-reflection

Although you'll find what appear to be contradictions among these quotes on knowing ourselves, seeing ourselves, and reflecting on our thoughts, words, choices and actions, there really are not. How we know ourselves may be different from how we appear in, and approach, our world. Self-knowledge is neither an easy, straight-lined march from youth to maturity, nor is it a moment-by-moment climb up a very rocky, slick cliff. It's both. It's more.

As you'll see within these quotes, there are many ways and many reasons to achieve self-knowledge and to realize our talents, strengths and gifts. At the same time, it is struggle -but an important one- to know our weaknesses and failings. And there's humor in gaining this knowledge of self. Like George Carlin said, "Don't sweat the petty things and don't pet the sweaty things."

~ ~ ~ ~

31. You are your best thing. — Toni Morrison

32. What you think, you become. —Guatama Buddha

33. Sometimes the longest journey we make is the sixteen inches from our heads to our hearts. — Elena Avila

34. Our preferences do not determine what's true. — Carl Sagan

35. Knowing yourself is the beginning of all wisdom. — Aristotle

36. Everyone leaves. Learn how to survive alone. — Anonymous

37. One must know oneself. If this does not serve to discover truth, it at least serves as a rule of life, and there is nothing better. — Blaise Pascal

38. Knowing others is intelligence; knowing yourself is true wisdom. — Lau Tzu

39. Talent is God-given, be humble. Fame is man-given, be thankful. Conceit is self-given, be careful. — John Wooden

40. It is not only the most difficult thing to know oneself, but the most inconvenient one, too. — H. W. Shaw

41. You can't laugh and be afraid at the same time…of anything. — Stephen Colbert

42. There are three things extremely hard: steel, a diamond, and to know one's self. — Benjamin Fraklin

43. When you know yourself you are empowered. When you accept yourself you are invincible. — Tina Lifford

44. The greatest discovery in life is self-discovery. Until you find yourself, you will always be someone else. Become yourself. — Myles Munroe

45. At the center of your being you have the answer; you know who you are and you know what you want. — Lao Tzu

46. Adventure can be an end in itself. Self-discovery is the secret ingredient that fuels daring, — Grace Lichtenstein

47. All the wonders you seek are within yourself. — Thomas Browne

48. Sometimes when you lose your way, you find yourself. — Mandy Hale

49. Don't get burned twice by the same flame. — Unknown

50. You've got to find yourself first. Everything else will follow. — Charles de Lint

51. I long, as does every human being, to be at home wherever I find myself. — Maya Angelou

52. Judge no one, just improve yourself. — Catch Smile

53. To be the best, you must be able to handle the worst. — Unknown

54. Self-awareness is the ability to take an honest look at your life without any attachment to it being right or wrong, good or bad. — Debbie Ford

55. Be obsessed with improving yourself. — Anonymous

56. The mystery of human existence lies not in just staying alive, but in finding something to live for. — Fyodor Dostoevsky

57. The two most important days in life are the day you were born and the day you find out why. — Mark Twain

58. Self-awareness allows you to self-correct.— Bill Hybels

59. Your struggle is part of your story. — Unknown

60. You were put on this earth to achieve your greatest self, to live out your purpose, and to do it courageously. — Steve Maraboli, *Life, the Truth, and Being Free*

61. Change the world by being yourself. — Amy Poehler

62. What consumes your mind, controls your life. — Ye Chen

63. Sometimes being alone is the best medicine to your soul. — Nicole Brown

64. Wanting to be someone else is a waste of who you are. — Kurt Cobain

65. Believe in yourself, take on your challenges, dig deep within yourself to conquer fears. Never let anyone bring you down. You got to keep going. — Chantal Sutherland

66. Be teachable. You're not always right. — Unknown

67. Everyone has been made for some particular work and the desire for that work has been put in every heart. — Jalaluddin Rumi

68. I haven't a clue how my story will end, but that's alright. When you set out on a journey, and night covers the road, that's when you discover the stars. — Nancy Willard

69. It is our choices that show what we truly are, far more than our abilities. — Unknown

70. Find people who will make you better. — Michelle Obama

71. Focus on improving yourself, not proving yourself. — Catch Smile

72. Your greatest asset in the world is your mindset. — Kenzi Kuo

73. Don't you know your imperfections are a blessing? — Kendrick Lamar

74. There is no greater gift you can give or receive than to honor your calling. It's why you were born. And how you become most truly alive. — Oprah Winfrey

75. Be yourself; everyone else is already taken. — Oscar Wilde

76. No one can make you feel inferior without your consent. — Eleanor Roosevelt

77. Learning to control and adjust your attitude to a positive one reflects the wisdom of the mind. — Catherine Pulsifer

78. You are at your strongest when you are calm. — Unknown

79. A man sooner or later discovers that he is the master gardener of his soul, the director of his life. — James Allen

80. Your relationship with yourself set the tone of every other relationship you have. — Robert Holden

81. Never react emotionally to criticism. Analyze yourself to determine whether it is justified. If it is,, correct yourself. Otherwise, go on about your business. — Norman Vincent Peale

82. Train your mind to see the good in everything. — Robin Guddat

83. Don't give up on yourself. There's a reason why you started. — *The Lyfe Magazine*

84. If I had known I was going to live this long, I would have taken better care of myself. — Mickey Mantle

85. Train your mind to be stronger than your feelings. — Unknown

86. You are never too old to set another goal or to dream a new dream. — Les Brown

87. Ask yourself: Will this matter a year from now? — Richard Carlson

88. Let me give you a wonderful Zen practice. Wake up in the morning, look in the mirror, and laugh at yourself. — Bernie Glassman

89. If you realize that you're the problem, then you can change yourself, learn something and grow wiser. Don't blame other people for your problems. — Robert Kiyosaki

90. We may look old and wise to the outside world, but to each other we are still in junior school. — Charlotte Gray

91. Be obsessed with becoming the best version of yourself. — Unknown

92. A boy is truth with dirt on its face, beauty with a cut on its finger, wisdom with bubble gum in its hair, and the hope of the future with a frog in its pocket. — Alan Beck

93. Hard times are sometimes blessings in disguise. We do have to suffer but in the end I makes us strong, better and wise. — Anurag Prakash Ray

94. I thought you loved me, but your actions say otherwise. If you love me, don't make me an option in your life — Unknown

95. Owning our story and loving ourselves through that process is the bravest thing we'll ever do. — Brene Brown

96. A girl might learn an ocean of wisdom from her mother, but having her father's presence is one part of the equation that should never be compromised. — Unknown

97. A new day: Be open enough to see opportunities. Be wise enough to be grateful. Be courageous enough to be happy. — Steve Maraboli

98. Knowing others is intelligence; knowing yourself is true wisdom. Mastering others is strength; mastering yourself is true power. — Laozi

99. It's a wise man who understands that every day is a new beginning, because boy, how many mistakes do you make in a day? — Mel Gibson

100. Self-awareness is knowing one's emotions. It is recognizing a feeling as it happens. — Daniel Goleman

101. I didn't fail the test. I just found 100 ways to do it wrong. — Benjamin Franklin

102. A vigorous five-mile walk will do more good for an unhappy but otherwise healthy adult than all the medicine and psychology in the world. — Paul Dudley White

103. Always watch where you are going. Otherwise, you may step on a piece of forest that was left out by mistake. — *Winnie the Pooh*

104. To free us from the expectations of others, to give us back to ourselves — there lies the great, the singular power of self-respect. — Joan Didion

105. I'm stronger because of the hard times, wiser because of my mistakes, and happier because I have known sadness. — Alison Vogel

106. He was swimming in a sea of other people's expectations. Men had drowned in seas like that. — Robert Jordan

107. You become the sum of your actions, and as you do, what flows from that — your impulses — reflect the actions you've taken. Choose wisely. — Ryan Holliday

108. I always had that self-belief that I was good enough. You have got to believe you are good enough, otherwise there is no point. — Glenn McGrath

109. Rise up, wise up, say it loud: Soul, I will not lie to you. I'm all alone, I'm still missing you, missing you, missing you. — Tegan Quin

110. The greatest discovery in life is self-discovery. Until you find yourself, you will always be someone else. Become yourself. — Myles Munroe

111. Everyone leaves; learn how to survive alone. — Anonymous

112. When you learn to survive without anyone, you can survive anything. — Jasmine

113. I, myself, enjoy my own company. The silence and calmness allow me to think. I love myself, we all should love ourselves, otherwise, who would we love? — Unknown

114. Be obsessed with improving yourself. — Anonymous

115. Whatever you are, be a good one. — Abraham Lincoln

~ ~ ~ ~

Francis E. Umesiri Quotes

116. The desire for meaning is stronger than the desire for pleasure. — Francis E. Umesiri

117. Your assignment is what you are called to do' your purpose is who you are called to be. —Francis E. Umesiri

118. The meaning of life is spiritual, so, to enjoy life, you must be spiritual too. — Francis E. Umesiri

119. Fulfilling your life's purpose and assignment depends on your ability to listen and respond accurately to the voice of wisdom within you. — Francis E. Umesiri

~ ~ ~ ~

Chapter Two

Your Fulfilled Life:

Fortitude and Freedom

How do you define fulfillment? Is freedom to do something the same as freedom to refuse to do something? Fortitude means "strength", but it's much more than that. Fortitude includes courage, determination, and stamina, but it also includes what the older generation calls "stick-to-it-iveness." Fulfillment is not only about what work you do, what salary you earn, or how high you've climbed the ladder of success.

At the same time, fulfillment, fortitude and freedom include our ability to accept, adapt to, and conquer what comedienne Gilda Radner called, "Delicious ambiguity."

Not only do these quotations focus on setting your goals, but also on how to achieve them, how to recognize the qualities it takes for realizing that achievement, and what criteria you choose to use for measuring your fulfillment in life. Even Hollywood legend Mae West weighs in here, letting you know that a sense of humor is part of the fulfillment process.

~ ~ ~ ~

120. Doing what you like is freedom, liking what you do is happiness. — Sudha Murty

121. True fulfillment comes from helping others. — Anonymous

122. Don't regret the past, just learn from it. — Ben Ipock

123. A goal without a plan is just a wish. — Antoine de Saint-Exuprey

124. Follow your heart. Trust your instincts and allow yourself to do what feels best. Above all, trust your wisdom within. — Laurie E. Smith

125. True success, true happiness lies in freedom and fulfillment. — Dada Vaswani

126. Far better it is to dare mighty things, to win glorious triumphs, even though checkered by failure, than to take rank with those poor spirits who neither enjoy much nor suffer much, because they live in the grey twilight that knows not victory nor defeat. — Theodore Roosevelt

127. Change will not come if we wait for some other person or some other time. We ae the ones we've been waiting for. We are the change that we seek. — Barrack Obama

128. You only live once, but if you do it right, once is enough. — Mae West

129. All the art of living lies in a fine mingling of letting go and holding on. — Henry Ellis

130. Losers visualize the penalties of failure. Winners visualize the rewards of success. — Unknown

131. Success without fulfillment is the ultimate failure. — Tony Robbins

132. Nobody who ever gave his best regretted it. — George Halas

133. Allow yourself to be a beginner — no one starts off being excellent. — Wendy Flynn

134. It is contentment that gives true fulfillment. — Anonymous

135. The whole problem with the world is that fools and fanatics are always so certain of themselves, and wiser people so full of doubts. — Bertrand Russell

136. It is not in the pursuit of happiness that we find fulfillment, it is in the happiness of pursuit. — Denis Waitley

137. Control your thoughts or your thoughts will control you. — Unknown

138. Whatever confronts you, don't believe it. When something appears shine your light on it. Have confidence in the light that is always working inside you. — Linji Yixuan

139. Keep in mind that you'll have true happiness, true fulfillment, not by living to get, but living to give. — Joel Osteen

140. Be wise because the world needs wisdom. If you cannot be wise, pretend to be someone who is wise, and then just behave like they would. — Neil Gaiman

141. A life directed toward the fulfillment of personal desires will sooner or later always lead to bitter disappointment. — Albert Einstein

142. Making progress in life is the biggest sense of fulfillment. — Anonymous

143. Success based on anything but internal fulfillment is bound to be empty. — Dr. Martha Friedman

144. The more intensely we feel about an idea or a goal, the more assuredly the idea, buried deep in our subconscious, will direct us along the path to its fulfillment. — Earl Nightingale

145. To have an extraordinary quality of life you need two skills: The science of achievement, and the art of fulfillment. — Tony Robbins

146. Creativity is an area in which younger people have a tremendous advantage, since they have an endearing habit of always questioning past wisdom and authority. — Bill Hewlett

147. Your long-term happiness and fulfillment depend on your ability to fulfill your soul's unique purpose

and to fill the place in the world that only you can fill, making the contribution that only you can make. — Red Stryker

148. The key to success and fulfillment in life starts with the awareness of and confidence in your own personal greatness. — Anonymous

149. Relationships based on selfish reasons will not give you love, fulfillment, or inner happiness. — Hina Hashmi

150. Loneliness is inner emptiness. Solitude is inner fulfillment. — Richard J. Foster

151. Occasionally in life there are those moments of unutterable fulfillment which cannot be completely explained by those symbols called words. Their meanings can only be articulated by the inaudible language of the heart. — Martin Luther King, Jr.

152. Don't confuse fun with fulfillment, or pleasure with happiness. — Michael Josephson

153. Happiness is a state of inner fulfillment. — Matthieu Ricard

154. We all have ability. The difference is how we use it. — Stevie Wonder

155. You will never grow to your fullest potential unless you plant seeds of joy, love, fulfillment, hope, and success. Nature can only return to you what you plant. — Anonymous

156. Life isn't about getting and having, it's about giving and being. — Kevin Kruse

157. Don't be defined by someone else's standards, have your own definition of success. — Duke Matlock

158. True happiness is a state of fulfillment. — Ashish Sophat

159. The art of fulfillment is the ability to experience not only the thrill of the chase but also the magic of the moment, the unbridled joy of feeling truly alive. — Tony Robbins

160. I think instead of happiness, we should be working for contentment, and inner sense of fulfillment that's relatively independent of external circumstances. — Andrew Weil

161. True fulfillment comes from helping others. — Anonymous

162. Life…is about not knowing, having to change, taking the moment and making the best of it, without knowing what's going to happen next. Delicious ambiguity. — Gilda Radner

163. Being alone has a power that very few people can handle. — Steven Atchison

164. There is no growth without pain. — Mark Manson

165. True success, true happiness lies in freedom and fulfillment. — Dada Vaswani

166. It is contentment that gives true fulfillment. — Anonymous

167. The art of fulfillment is the ability to experience not only the thrill of the chase but also the magic of the moment, the unbridled joy of feeling truly alive. —Tony Robbins

168. True happiness is a state of fulfillment. — Ashish Sophat

169. Allow yourself to be a beginner - no one starts off being excellent. —Wendy Flynn

170. A life directed chiefly toward the fulfillment of personal desires will sooner or later always lead to bitter disappointment. —Albert Einstein

171. Keep in mind that you'll have true happiness, true fulfillment, not living to get but living to give.— Joel Osteen

172. You will never grow to your fullest potential unless you plant seeds of joy, love, fulfillment, hope,

173. and success. Nature can only return to you what you plant. —Anonymous

174. Happiness is a state of inner fulfillment. — Matthieu Ricard

175. Life isn't about getting and having, it's about giving and being. — Kevin Kruse

176. Success without fulfillment is the ultimate failure. —Tony Robbins

177. Your long-term happiness and fulfillment depend on your ability to fulfill your soul's unique purpose and to fill the place in the world that only you can fill, making the contribution that only you can make. — Rod Stryker

178. The more intensely we feel about an idea or a goal, the more assuredly the idea, buried deep in our subconscious, will direct us along the path to its fulfillment. — Earl Nightingale

179. To have an extraordinary quality of life you need two skills: the science of achievement and the art of fulfillment. —Tony Robbins

180. The key to success and fulfillment in life starts with the awareness of and confidence in your own personal greatness. — Anonymous

181. A negative mind will never give you a positive life. — Ziad K. Abdelnour

~ ~ ~ ~

Quotes of Stephen Covey

182. Where we stand depends on where we sit. Each of us tends to think we see things as they are, that we are objective. But this is not the case. We see the world, not as it is, but as we are — or, as we are conditioned to see it. When we open our mouths to describe what we see, we in effect describe ourselves, our perceptions, our paradigms. When other people disagree with us, we immediately think something is wrong with them. —Stephen Covey

183. If I were to summarize in one sentence the single most important principle I have learned in the field of interpersonal relations, it would be this: Seek first to understand, then to be understood. — Stephen Covey

184. The key is not to prioritize what's on your schedule, but to schedule your priorities. — Stephen Covey

185. But until a person can say deeply and honestly, 'I am what I am today because of the choices I made yesterday,' that person cannot say, 'I choose otherwise. — Stephen R. Covey

186. The main thing is to keep the main thing the main thing. — Stephen Covey

187. Most of us spend too much time on what is urgent and not enough time on what is important. — Stephen Covey

188. I am not a product of my circumstances. I am a product of my decisions. — Stephen Covey

189. You have to decide what your highest priorities are and have the courage — pleasantly, smilingly, non-apologetically, to say "no" to other things. And the way you do that is by having a bigger "yes" burning inside. The enemy of the "best" is often the "good. — Stephen Covey

190. I teach people how to treat me by what I will allow. —Stephen Covey

191. Live, love, laugh, leave a legacy.   Stephen Covey

192. Be patient with yourself. Self-growth is tender; it's holy ground. There's no greater investment — Stephen Covey

193. Live out of your imagination, not your history. —Stephen Covey

194. Humility is the mother of all virtues, courage the father, integrity the child and wisdom the grandchild. —Stephen Covey

195. Trust is the glue of life. It's the most essential ingredient in effective communication. It's the foundational principle that holds all relationships. — Stephen Cove

Chapter Three

Your Words: Say What you

Mean and Mean What you Say

LOL, TMI, OMG. Are those words? They each convey a message. In the fewest letters possible. But if you text your BFF, he or she will get your message. When it comes to meaning, three letters may not be enough. When it comes to making a point and ensuring it is clearly understood, a text message may not suffice.

We sometimes try to think of a word or expression and we say "it's on the tip of my tongue." When we have trouble communicating, we say we're "tongue-tied." When we utter the wrong word at the wrong time, it's "a slip of the tongue." It's impossible to know how many words there are in any given language because words are added and meanings change. Back in the day, "swipe" meant to take something that didn't belong to you. Now, "swipe" is what we do with our credit or debit cards.

Whether it's work, learning and academics, recreation, or even prayer, what we say to others does matter; we can't crawl inside their heads to make sure they "got" what we meant from the words we uttered or wrote. In parenting, a frequent refrain from our children is: "But you *said* we could!" As parents or teachers, mentors and leaders, it's common to say, "Do as I *say,* not as I do."

As someone once said, silence is often the best answer to a query or statement. "Reading between the lines" is an art form all its own. Words matter. Spelling matters. Speech matters. Writing matters, even if it's a three-letter text message. Yet, "actions speak louder than words," may be an ultimate truth, just like the saying that we have two ears and one mouth so we can listen twice as much as we say anything. Words hurt, heal, help, humor, and honor. Choose and use your words carefully: say what you mean and mean what you say, out loud or silently.

~ ~ ~ ~

196. If you tell the truth you don't have to remember anything. —Mark Twain

197. The way you speak to yourself matters the most. — Jessica Lutz, *Forbes*

198. One who does what he says is not a coward. — African proverb

199. Words are like keys; if you choose them right, they can open any heart and shut any mouth. — Unknown

200. Before you act, listen. Before you react, think. Before you spend, earn. Before you criticize, wait. Before you pray, forgive. Before you quit, try. — William Arthur Ward

201. Have enough courage to start and enough heart to finish. — Jessica N. S. Yourko

202. When you build in silence, people don't know what to attack. —Unknown

203. Grant me the courage to serve others; for in service there is true life. — Cesar Chavez

204. Silence is the best answer to someone who doesn't value your words. —Unknown

205. You get treated in life the way you teach people to treat you. — Wayne Dyer

206. The quieter you become the more you can hear. —Rumi

207. The most important thing in communication is hearing what isn't being said. The art of reading between the lines is a lifelong quest of the wise. — Shannon L. Adler

208. Move in silence. Only speak when it's time to say "checkmate." —Lorenzo Senni

209. I would rather die of passion than of boredom. — Vincent van Gogh

210. Nothing is easier than saying words. Nothing is harder than living them, day after day. —Arthur Gordon

211. Your only limit: words without action be.— Anonymous

212. If you're offered a seat on a rocket ship, don't ask what seat! Just get on. — Sheryl Sandberg

213. Life is like a coin. You can spend it any way you wish, but you only spend it once. — Lillian Dickson

214. I write only when inspiration strikes. Fortunately, it strikes every morning at nine o'clock sharp. — W. Somerset Maugham

215. I want to write because I have the urge to excel in one medium of translation and expression of life.

I can't be satisfied with the colossal job of merely living. — Sylvia Plath

216. You can't always expect people to apply your wisdom when they didn't use wisdom before they found themselves knee deep in their version of justice. — Sharon L. Alder

217. Our preferences do not determine what's true. — Carl Sagan

218. You have and will live an amazing life ahead. I pray God gives you the wisdom needed to make the right choices. Happiest 70th birthday. — Unknown

219. How wonderful it is that nobody need wait a single moment before starting to improve the world. — Anne Frank, *Diary*

220. The book or the music in which we thought the beauty was located will betray us if we trust to them; it was not in them, it only came through them… For they are not the thing itself: they are only the scent of the flower we have not found, the echo of a tune we have not heard, news from a country we have not visited. — C. S. Lewis

221. Aspire to inspire before you expire. — Eugene Bell, Jr.

222. In three words I can sum up everything I've learned about life: it goes on. —Robert Frost

223. While this quote may make you smile this Tuesday, it is one that contains words of wisdom as you work towards your goals!— Anonymous

224. Life is short and it is here to be lived. — Kate Winslett

225. Never be bullied into silence. Never allow yourself to be made a victim. Accept no one's definition of your life but define yourself. — Harvey S. Firestone

226. Every day is a new beginning. Treat it that way. Stay away from what might have been and look at what can be. — Marsha Petrie Sue

227. What consumes your mind controls your life. — Ye Chen

228. When I was ten, I read fairy tales in secret and would have been ashamed if I had been found doing so. Now that I am fifty, I read them openly. When I became a man I put away childish things, including the fear of childishness and the desire to be very grown up. — C. S. Lewis

229. If I waited for perfection, I would never write a word. — Margaret Atwood

230. The way you speak to yourself matters the most. — Jessica Lutz, *Forbes*

231. I think everybody should get rich and famous and do everything they ever dreamed of so they can see that it's not the answer. — Jim Carrey

232. I read a book one day and my whole life was changed. — Orhan Pamuk

233. I've learned that people will forget what you said, people will forget what you did, but people will never forget how you made them feel. —Maya Angelou

234. Slang is a language that rolls up its sleeves, spits on its hands, and gets to work. — Carl Sandburg

235. Few people have the wisdom to prefer the criticism that would do them good to the praise that deceives them. — Francis de La Rochefoucauld

236. Recognize your impact, regardless od your intent. Say, "I'm sorry", mean it and be better. It's that simple. — Mandy Manning

237. Sometimes in life, under the stress of an exceptional emotion, people *do* say what they think. — Marcel Proust

238. If you don't like something, change it; if you can't change it, change the way you think about it. — Mary Engelbreit

239. Let people doubt your sanity. Let them think you're nuts. Be the mad scientist, the wise fool, the adventure addict who makes others question their own aliveness. — Amy McTear

240. Music is your own experience, your thoughts, your wisdom. If you don't live it, it won't come out of you. — Charlie "Bird" Parker

241. Self-pity is our worst enemy and if we yield to it, we can never do anything wise in the world. — Helen Keller

242. If a man devotes himself to art, much evil is avoided that happens otherwise if on is ide. — Albrecht Durer

243. The wise try to adjust themselves to the truth, while fools try to adjust the truth to themselves. — Thibault

244. In complete darkness, we are all the same, it is only our knowledge and wisdom that separate us; don't let your eyes deceive you. — Janet Jackson

245. It is better to love wisely, no doubt; but to love foolishly is better than not to be able to love at all. — William Makepeace Thackery

~ ~ ~ ~

Dale Carnegie Quotes:

246. It isn't what you have or who you are or where you are or what you are doing that makes you happy or unhappy. It is what you think about it. — Dale Carnegie

247. Don't be afraid of enemies who attack you. Be afraid of the friends who flatter you. — Dale Carnegie, *How to Win Friends and Influence People*

248. Develop success from failures. Discouragement and failure are two of the surest stepping stones to success. —Dale Carnegie

249. You can make more friends in two months by becoming interested in other people than you can in two years by trying to get other people interested in you.—Dale Carnegie, *How to Win Friends and Influence People*

250. Any fool can criticize, complain, and condemn—and most fools do. But it takes character and self-control to be understanding and forgiving. —Dale Carnegie, *How to Win Friends and Influence People*

251. When dealing with people, remember you are not dealing with creatures of logic, but with creatures bristling with prejudice and motivated by pride and vanity. — Dale Carnegie, *How to Win Friends and Influence People*

252. Success is getting what you want. Happiness is wanting what you get. — Dale Carnegie

253. Everybody in the world is seeking happiness—and there is one sure way to find it. That is by controlling your thoughts. Happiness doesn't depend on outward conditions. It depends on inner conditions. — Dale Carnegie, *How to Win Friends and Influence People*

254. When we hate our enemies, we are giving them power over us: power over our sleep, our appetites, our blood pressure, our health, and our happiness." — Dale Carnegie, *How to Stop Worrying and Start Living*

255. Most of the important things in the world have been accomplished by people who have kept on trying when there seemed to be no hope at all. — Dale Carnegie

256. Inaction breeds doubt and fear. Action breeds confidence and courage. If you want to conquer fear, do not sit home and think about it. Go out and get busy. — Dale Carnegie

257. People rarely succeed unless they have fun in what they are doing. — Dale Carnegie

258. Remember, today is the tomorrow you worried about yesterday. — Dale Carnegie

259. Talk to someone about themselves and they'll listen for hours. — Dale Carnegie, *How to Win Friends and Influence People*

260. If you want to gather honey, don't kick over the beehive — Dale Carnegie

261. If you are not in the process of becoming the person you want to be, you are automatically engaged in becoming the person you don't want to be. — Dale Carnegie

262. Be wiser than other people if you can; but do not tell them so. — Dale Carnegie

263. Actions speak louder than words, and a smile says, 'I like you. You make me happy. I am glad to see you.' That is why dogs make such a hit. They are so glad to see us that they almost jump out of their skins. So, naturally, we are glad to see them. — Dale Carnegie, *How to Win Friends and Influence People*

264. Even God doesn't propose to judge a man till his last days, why should you and I? — Dale Carnegie

265. Our thoughts make us what we are. — Dale Carnegie, *How to Stop Worrying and Start Living*

266. Knowledge isn't power until it is applied. — Dale Carnegie

267. The best possible way to prepare for tomorrow is to concentrate with all your intelligence, all your enthusiasm, on doing today's work superbly today. That is the only possible way you can prepare for the future. — Dale Carnegie, *How to Stop Worrying and Start Living*

268. No matter what happens, always be yourself. — Dale Carnegie, *How to Stop Worrying and Start Living*

269. Be more concerned with your character than with your reputation, for your character is what you are, while your reputation is merely what others think you are. — Dale Carnegie

270. You can't win an argument. You can't because if you lose it, you lose it; and if you win it, you lose it. — Dale Carnegie, *How to Win Friends and Influence People*

271. If you can't sleep, then get up and do something instead of lying there and worrying. It's the worry that gets you, not the loss of sleep. — Dale Carnegie

272. One reason why birds and horses are not unhappy is because they are not trying to impress other birds and horses. — Dale Carnegie

273. A man convinced against his will is of the same opinion still. — Dale Carnegie, *How to Win Friends and Influence People*

274. To be interesting, be interested. — Dale Carnegie, *How to Win Friends and Influence People*

~ ~ ~

Chapter Four

Gratitude, Grit and Relationships

How successful, happy, wealthy and wise would we be if we believed we did it all on our own? Frank Sinatra sang, "I did it my way." Some people make it clear that it's "my way or the highway." In truth, we could not reach our goals without other people.

It's fine to believe in yourself and your many assets, but we all live in a world filled with other people: Some we will never meet; some we will never know; some we will never acknowledge; some we will never notice, some we will see but not "see." Among all those other people, though, are the ones who see us as we are and see all we do in the clearest light. Some people may hate us; some may bully and make fun of us; some will betray us; some will be our champions, cheerleaders, and compadres. Through this world of other people, we make our way, and when we succeed, we need to not only recognize those who helped us (in good or challenging ways), as well as those who are coming after us that need our help, guidance, enthusiasm, and steadfast support.

Sometimes we're right; sometimes we're not. Sometimes we make it; sometimes we don't. Goals may explode before our eyes. Relationships may flourish or founder. We may feel 100% that we are in this world, this moment, alone, but those who succeed learn the sweet is better after the bitter, and the prize is more powerful after we weathered defeat before trying again.

~ ~ ~ ~

275. Far better it is to dare mighty things, to win glorious triumphs, even though checkered by failure, than to take rank with those poor spirits who neither enjoy much nor suffer much, because they live in the grey twilight that knows not victory nor defeat. — Theodore Roosevelt

276. When someone is in your heart, they're never truly gone. They can come back to you, even at unlikely times. — Mitch Albom

277. Never make a permanent decision based on temporary feelings. — Unknown

278. Change will not come if we wait for some other person or some other time. We are the ones we've been waiting for. We are the change that we seek. — Barack Obama

279. In all of living, have much fun and laughter. Life is to be enjoyed, not just endured. — Gordon B. Hinckley

280. Kindness is more important than wisdom, and the recognition of this is the beginning of wisdom. — Theodore Rohn

281. The greatest wisdom lies on the other side, immediately on the other side, of the greatest despair. — Alan Watts

282. Grief can be the garden of compassion. If you keep your heart open through everything, your pain can become your greatest ally in your life' search for love and wisdom. — Rumi

283. I didn't think you can cheat on a person you love and if you do, you never loved them fully, otherwise there wouldn't be any voids to fill. — Unknown

284. Focus on improving yourself, not proving yourself. — Unknown

285. I long, as does every human being, to be at home wherever I find myself. — Maya Angelou

286. We must be willing to let go of the life we've planned, so as to have the life that is waiting for u. — Joseph Campbell

287. If you are not willing to risk the usual, you will have to settle for the ordinary. — Jim Rohn

288. Believe you can and you're halfway there. — Theodore Roosevelt

289. In playing ball, and in life, a person occasionally gets the opportunity to do something great. When that time comes, only two things matter: being prepared to seize the moment, and having the courage to take your best swing. — Hank Aaron

290. Hard times are sometimes blessings in disguise. We do have to suffer, but in the end, it makes us strong, better, and wise. — Anurag Prakash Ray

291. I've learned that no matter what happens, or how bad it seems today, life does go on, and it will be better tomorrow. — Maya Angelou

292. Adversity causes some men to break, and others to break records. — Unknown

293. Life isn't about waiting for the storm to pass. It' about learning how to dance in the rain. — Vivian Greene

294. A strong woman builds her own world. She is one who is wise enough to know that it will attract the man she will gladly share it with. — Ellen Barrier

295. You can't reach what's in front of you until you let go of what's behind you. —Jessica Park, *180 Seconds*

296. Losers visualize the penalties of failure. Winners visualize the rewards of success. — Unknown

297. Don't be defined by someone else's standards, have your own definition of success. — Duke Matlock

298. Nobody who ever gave his best regretted it. — George Halas

299. Hope is like a road in the country; there was never a road but when many people walk on it, the road comes into existence. — Lin Yutang

300. Success based on anything but internal fulfillment is bound to be empty. — Dr. Martha Friedman

301. Take criticism seriously, but not personally. If there is truth or merit in the criticism, try to learn from it. Otherwise, let it roll right off you. — Hillary Clinton

302. As long as you are alive, no obstacle is permanent. — Unknown

303. Sacrifice a few years of comfort for decades of freedom. — Zach Pogorob

304. What I can tell you is that with the exception of the wit and wisdom of *Calvin and Hobbes*, not much lasts forever. — Ted Lasso

305. When it comes to life the critical thing is, whether you take things for granted or take them with gratitude. — Gilbert Chesterton

306. Change the world by being yourself. — Amy Poehler

307. Give love to all; hatred to none. — Hazrat Mirsa Nasir Ahmad

308. Only a fool learns from his own mistakes. The wise man learns from the mistakes of others. — Otto von Bismarck

309. When we seek to discover the best in others, we somehow bring out the best in ourselves. — William Arthur Ward

310. Have patience — all things are difficult before they become easy. — Saachi

311. The quickest way to rectify that mistake (choosing the wrong person) is by learning from that, moving on, and choosing much more wisely in the future. — Greg Behrendt

312. Being loyal to someone is a good thing…when it's reciprocated. Otherwise, you are only being their fool. — Unknown

313. We should set our goals; then learn to control our appetites. Otherwise, we will lose ourselves in the confusion of the world. — Hark Herald Samiento

314. If you keep your heart open through everything, your pain can become your greatest ally in your life's search for love and wisdom. — Rumi

315. Hardship often prepares an ordinary person for an extraordinary destiny. — Christopher Markus

316. You know how to cut to the core of me, Baxter. You're so wise. You're like a miniature Buddha, covered with hair. — *Ron Burgundy, Anchorman*

317. You make every day in this place so much brighter. Thank you for all of your wit and wisdom. You will be greatly missed. — Unknown

318. Find someone who has a life that you want and figure out how they got it. Read books, pick your role models wisely. Find out what they did and do it. — Lana del Rey

319. You are a sister of the heart. I'm so grateful for you. They always say that the teacher appears when you are ready. Thank you for your love and wisdom. — Lisa Marie Selow

320. It's Pollyannaish not to express your feelings when someone has done something wrong. But it must be done tactfully; otherwise, your criticism will be destructive. — Mary Kay Ash

321. It is strange how often a heart must be broken, before the years can make it wise. — Sara Teasdale, *The Collected Poems*

322. When you cease to dream, you cease to live. — Malcolm Forbes

323. You do not find the happy life. You make it. — Camilla Eyring Kimball

324. Our own worst enemy cannot harm us as much as our unwise thoughts. No one can help us as much as our won compassionate thoughts. — Buddha

325. Gratitude opens the door to the power, the wisdom, the creativity of the universe. You open the door through gratitude. —Deepak Chopra

326. Avoid those who seek friends in order to maintain a certain social status or to open doors they would not otherwise be able to approach. — Paulo Coelho

327. Relationships based on selfish reasons will not give you love, fulfillment or inner-happiness. —Hina Hashmi

328. No one reaches out to you for compassion or empathy so you can teach them how to behave better. They reach out because they believe in our capacity to know our darkness well enough to sit in the dark with them. — Brene Brown

329. May the good lord bless you with longevity, wisdom, peace of mind, and bliss. Happy six months birthday, my darling. — Unknown

330. Loneliness is inner emptiness. Solitude is inner fulfillment. — Richard J. Foster

331. The human heart is the only thing whose worth increases the more it is broken. — Shakieb Orgunwall

332. Don't confuse fun with fulfillment, or pleasure with happiness. — Michael Josephson

333. Mind your own business; the best statement that any wise person can see as encouragement and best advice ever. — Unarine Ramaru

334. The main problem with this great obsession for saving time is very simple: You can't save time. You can only spend it. But you can spend it wisely or foolishly. — Benjamin Franklin

335. If you want to be happy, be. — Leo Tolstoy

336. Good social relationships are like food and thermoregulation, universally important to human mood. — Martin Seligman

337. Time is like oxygen — there is a minimum amount that's necessary for survival. And it takes quantity as well as quality to develop warm and caring relationships. — Armand Nicholi

338. Relationships help us to define who we are and what we can become. Most of us can trace our success to pivotal relationships. — Donald O. Clifton & Paula Nelson

339. To the person who invented zero: Thanks for nothing. — Unknown

340. Beauty is not who you are on the outside, it is the wisdom and time you gave away to save another struggling soul like you. — Shannon Alder

341. Kindness is more important than wisdom, and the recognition of this is the beginning of wisdom. — Theodore Isaac Rubin

342. Your mind will keep you up at night, make you cry, destroy you over and over again. You need to convince your mind that it has to let go — because your heart already knows how to heal. — Nikita Gill

343. Occasionally in life there are those moments of unutterable fulfillment which cannot be completely explained by those symbols called words. Their meanings can only be articulated by the inaudible language of the heart. — Martin Luther King, Jr.

344. Do it alone. Do it broke. Do it tired. Do it scared. Just do it. —Office Essentials

345. Making progress in life is the biggest sense of fulfillment. — Anonymous

346. Courage is the power to let go of the familiar. — Raymond Lindquist

347. Dear daughter, life is short. Spend it wisely by doing things that would put a smile on your face. Happy birthday, sweetheart. — Unknown

348. I keep my friends as misers keep their treasure, because, of all the things granted to us by wisdom, noe is greater or better than friendship. — Pietro Aretino

349. I think instead of happiness, we should be working for contentment, and inner sense of fulfillment that's relatively independent of external circumstances. —Andrew Weil

350. No one who achieves success does so without the help of others. The wise and confident acknowledge this help with gratitude. — Alfred North Whitehead

351. I believe that what we become depends on what our fathers teach us at odd moments when they aren't trying to teach us. We are formed by little scraps of wisdom. — Umberto Eco

352. Don't wish it was easier, wish you were better. Don't wish for less problems, wish for more skills. And don't wish for less challenge, wish for more wisdom. — Jim Rohn

353. Happy birthday, my Daddy, who does so much for everyone I our family. Your wisdom, compassion, and strength serve as an inspiration to all of us. — Unknown

354. A teacher is a compass that activates the magnets of curiosity, knowledge, and wisdom in pupils. — Ever Garrison

355. Happy Thursday! Greet your problems and decisions with peace and calm. Use your inner wisdom to evaluate and make smart decisions for yourself. You got this! — Unknown

356. Having a grateful disposition brings about other virtues, including generosity, compassion, humility, joy, wisdom, trust, and integrity. — Howard Cosell

357. If you're luck enough to find a weirdo, never let them go. A big happy birthday yo my weirdo, who's another year older but not wiser. — Unknown

358. If you look to others for fulfillment, you will never be truly fulfilled. — Lao Tzu

359. Make this a year of finding fulfillment, joy, peace, and purpose. — Anonymous

360. Don't cry because it's over; smile because it happened. —Dr. Seuss

361. Today is special. I am a little stronger and wiser than the previous year. In this coming year, I promise myself to make the best out of it. — Unknown

362. No wise man ever wished to be younger. Celebrate, cheer, sing, eat, and laugh the day away. —Jonathan Swift

363. Even more than the time when she gave birth, a mother feels her greatest joy when she hears others refer to her son as a wise learned one. — Thiruvalluvar

364. Be selfish with your time, a lot of people don't deserve it. —Unknown

365. If you only walk on sunny days, you'll never reach your destination. —Paulo Coelho

366. Fear is temporary; regret is forever. —Ashley Pruitt

367. The saying goes that wisdom is not measured in years. Well, you've had 70 years of experience, and I think that adds up to quite a lot of wisdom. — Unknown

368. He was swimming in a sea of other people's expectations. Men have drowned in seas like that. — Robert Jordan

369. A man with wisdom will always have a solution, no matter how big his challenges may be. Wisdom makes you a problem solver. — Patience Johnson

370. It is strange how often a heart must be broken. Before the years can make it wise. — Sara Teasdale, *The Collected Poems.*

~ ~ ~ ~

Mike Murdoch quotes:

371. Every problem in your life is simply a wisdom problem. — Mike Murdoch

372. When your heart decides the destination, your mind will design the map to reach it. — Mike Murdoch

373. What you respect you will attract. — Mike Murdoch

374. The secret of your future is hidden in your daily routine. — Mike Murdoch

375. Your rewards in life are determined by the problems you are willing to solve for others. — Mike Murdoch

~ ~ ~ ~

Chapter Five

Success, Failure,

Mistakes, and Resilience

As the saying goes, "Success is never owned, it's rented." Books, podcasts, articles, and even movies have been created around the idea of success, but many people are hard-pressed to define the word. Is success something you deserve? Can you earn it? Can it fall into your lap? Is success a destination where, once you arrive there, you've got it made?

Failure is an equally-weighty concept and we tend to believe it is the opposite of success. But is failure a personal trait, the luck of the draw, a punishment for our actions? Is making mistakes the same as failing? After all, Benjamin Franklin was an exceptional individual and he once stated, "I didn't fail the test. I just found 100 ways to do it wrong."

Often, we find or achieve success in one area of our lives but have failed in other areas. To keep going, day-by-day requires resilience, or the ability to move forward despite facing adversity, failure, mistreatment, or injustice. Here, we have quotes about success, failure, mistakes and resilience, all of which can intertwine in our lives. Success, failure, mistakes and resilience may have marked our past; perhaps we've learned from them. Regardless, we will surely encounter — even create — one or more of those conditions in the future.

376. Success is not failure; failure is not fatal. It is the courage to continue that counts. — Winston Churchill

377. You don't need more time — you need less distractions. — Unknown

378. What's the key to success? The key is, there is not key. Be humble, hungry, and the hardest worker in any room. — Dwayne "the Rock" Johnson

379. A successful man is one who can lay a firm foundation with the bricks that others throw at him. — David Brinkley

380. Success is not an accident. It is hard work, perseverance, learning, studying, sacrifice, and most of all, love of what you are doing. — Pele

381. There is no growth without pain. — Mark Manson

382. Look forward with hope not backwards with regret. — Unknown

383. The moment when you want to quit is the moment when you need to keep pushing. — Paulo Coelho

384. Turn the pain into power. — Peter Liss, *Psychology Today*

385. A goal without a plan is just a wish. — Antoine de Saint-Exuprey

386. Don't blame the distractions. Improve your focus. — Unknown

387. Failure is the greatest teacher. — Deepak Ohri; Yoda, et al.

388. Don't call it problems, instead, call it challenges. — Unknown

389. The only impossible journey is the one you never begin. — Tony Robbins

390. Do your best when no one is looking. If you do that, then you can be successful in anything that you put your mind to. — Bob Cousy

391. High achievement always takes place in the framework of high expectations. — Charles F. Kettering

392. You can't let your failures define you — you have to let them teach you. You let them show you what to do differently next time. — Barrack Obama

393. Better days are coming; be patient. — Anonymous

394. Don't quit. Nothing lasts forever, not even pain. — *Absolute Motivation*

395. Improvise, adapt, overcome. — the Green Berets

396. No regrets in life — just lessons learned. — Ed Lapiz

397. If you can stay positive in a negative situation, you win. — Mark Allen Williams

398. Doubt kills more dreams than failure ever will. — Suzy Kassem

399. You only fail when you stop trying. — Unknown

400. Worry is like a rocking chair; it gives you something to do but never gets you anywhere. — Erma Bombeck

401. Envy blinds men and makes it impossible for them to think clearly. — Malcolm X

402. What is important is ideas. If you have ideas, you have the main asset you need, and there isn't any limit to what you can do with your business and your life. — Harvey Firestone

403. You have to pay the price. You will find that everything in life exacts a price, and you will have to decide whether the price is worth the prize. — Sam Nunn

404. All progress is based upon a universal innate desire on the part of every living organism to live beyond its income. — Samuel Butler

405. I promise there'll be a tomorrow...in fact, it's already tomorrow in Australia. — Charles M. Schulz

406. Excuses make today easy, but they make tomorrow hard. Discipline makes today hard, but it makes tomorrow easy. — Michael Oher

407. Don't take life too seriously; you'll never get out of it alive. — Elbert Hubbard

408. You've gotta dance like there's nobody watching; love like you've never been hurt; sing like there's nobody listening and live like it's heaven on earth. — Willaim W. Purkey

409. We fall, we break, we fail. But then we rise, we heal, we overcome. — Unknown

410. Without rain nothing grows. Learn to embrace the storm of your life. — Anonymous

411. Don't let yesterday take up too much of today. — John Wooden

412. If you're tired, learn to rest, not to quit. — Banksy

413. Failure is only a temporary change in direction to set you straight for your next success. — Denis Waitley

414. The biggest adventure you can ever take is to live the life of your dreams. — Oprah Winfrey

415. Right actions for the future are the best apologies for wrong ones in the past. — Tryon Edwards

416. Life has many different chapters for us. One bad chapter doesn't mean it's the end of the book. — Edenia Archuleta

417. Sometimes I win, sometimes I learn, but I never lose. — John C. Williams

418. Fix your thoughts, fix your life. — Unknown

419. If you put yourself in a position where you have to stretch outside your comfort zone, then you are forced to expand your consciousness. — Les Brown

420. Train your mind to be calm in every situation. — Unknown

421. It's said that a wise person learns from his mistakes. A wiser one learns from others' mistakes. But the wisest person of all learns from others' successes. — John C. Maxwell

422. Don't be distracted by criticism. Remember — the only taste of success some people get is to take a bite out of you. — Zig Ziglar

423. There are no secrets to success. It is the result of preparation, hard work, and learning from failure. — Colin Powell

424. The real test is not whether you avoid this failure, because you won't. It's whether you let it harden or shame you into inaction, or whether you learn from it; whether you choose to persevere. — Barrack Obama

425. It is better to fail in originality than to succeed in imitation. — Herman Melville

426. The road to success and the road to failure area almost exactly the same. — Colin R. Davis

427. Always remember, your focus determines your reality. — George Lucas

428. Success is walking from failure to failure with no loss of enthusiasm. — Winston Churchill

429. If you genuinely want something, don't wait for it. Teach yourself to be impatient. — Gurbaksh Chahal

430. The only place where success comes before work is in the dictionary. —Vidal Sassoon

431. If you can dream it, you can do it. — Walt Disney

432. The secret of success is learning how to use pain and pleasure instead of having pain and pleasure use you. If you do that, you're in control of your life. If you don't life controls you. — Tony Robbins

433. If you don't have time to do it right, when will you have time to do it again? — John Wooden

434. Just because your mind tells you that something is awful or evil or unplanned or otherwise negative doesn't mean you have to agree. — Ryan Holliday

435. A good man and a wise man may at times be angry with the world, at times grieved for it; but be sure no man was ever discontented with the world who did his duty in it. — Robert Southey

436. The difference between who you are and what you want to be is what you do. — Denis Waitley

437. Growth doesn't happen in your comfort zone. — Jocko Willink

438. Accept what is. Let go of what was. Have faith in what will be. — Catherine Galasso-Vigorito

439. When we got into office, the thing that surprised me the most was to find that things were just as bad as we'd been saying they were. — John F. Kennedy

440. A very wise man once told me that you can't look back — you just have to put the past behind you and find something better in your future. — Joseph Campbell

441. Accept what you can't change. Change what you can't accept. — Angela Davis

442. To begin to think with purpose is to enter the ranks of those strong ones who only recognize failure as one of the pathways to attainment. — James Allen

443. By setting and pursuing goals, you have nothing to lose but a lot to gain. It has been scientifically proven that people who set goals are more fulfilled and positive about life. Having a purpose to wake up to each day will challenge us and give us meaning. — Zoe McKey

444. Put all your energy into watering one area. If you spread the water across many seeds, you don' have as much water for one seed. Focus on one thing. Make it your priority. — Unknown

445. Perhaps the single most important ingredient in all of life for achieving happiness and fulfillment: Purpose. — Harvey Volson

446. There are no mistakes in life, only lessons. There is no such thing as a negative experience, only opportunities to grow, learn, an advance along the road of self-mastery. From struggle comes strength. Even pain can be a wonderful teacher. — Robin Sharma

447. If you set your goals ridiculously high and it's a failure, you will fail above everyone else's success. — James Cameron

448. If you want to make your dreams come true, the first thing you have to do is wake up. — J. M. Power

449. Succes usually comes to those who are too busy to be looing for it. — Henry David Thoreau

450. Many of life's failures are people who did not realize how close they were to success when they gave up. — Thomas A. Edison

451. You miss 100% of the shots you don't take. — Wayne Gretzky

452. With great power comes great responsibility. — Stan Lee

453. Whatever the mind of man can conceive and believe, it can achieve. — Napoleon Hill

454. Days are expensive. When you spend a day you have one less day to spend. So make sure you spend each one wisely. — Jim Rohn

455. Never reveal what you have thought upon doing, but by wise counsel keep it secret, being determined to carry it into execution. — Chanakya

456. You become the sum of your actions, and as you do, what flows from that — your impulses-reflect the actions you've taken. Choose wisely. — Ryan Holliday

457. Hard times may have put you down sometimes but they will not last forever. When all is said and done, you will be wise and strong. — Anurag Prakash Ray

458. Learning allows for more wisdom and knowledge, Additional knowledge about any situation increases the strength of an opinion. — Faye Horton

459. Power is not what we do but what we do not - hasty and unwise actions that we repeat every day and which ultimately bring us into trouble. — Robert Greene

460. Yesterday I was clever, so to change the world. Today I am wise, so I am changing myself. — Jalaluddin Rumi

461. You will make some mistakes, but if you learn from those mistakes, those mistakes will become wisdom and wisdom is essential to becoming wealthy. — Robert Kiyosaki

462. Till now poets were privileged to insert a certain proportion of nonsense — very far in excess of one half of one per cent — into their otherwise sober documents. — John Crowe Ransom

463. In any given moment we have two options: to step forward into growth or to step back into safety. — Abraham Maslow

464. You must take personal responsibility. You cannot change the circumstances, the seasons, or the wind, but you can change yourself. That is something you have charge of. — Jim Rohn

465. If we hold onto our own ideas of how things should be rather than accepting how they really are, we arise conflict in ourselves in the form of defensiveness. — Carl Rogers

466. We should accept our negative feelings rather than avoid or repress them. Suffering contributes to psychological growth. — Rollo May

467. To turn natural sadness into depression, all you have to do is blame yourself for the disaster that has befallen you. — Dorothy Rowe

468. Nothing is so painful to the human mind as a great and sudden change. — Mary Wollstonecraft Shelley

469. To know how to grow old is the masterwork of wisdom, and one of the most difficult chapters in the great art of living. —Henri Frederic Amiel

470. I wish for you the wisdom to realize it's okay to miss something, but not want it back. — Steve Maraboli

471. Before beginning a hunt, it is wise to ask someone what you are looking for before you begin looking for it. — Winnie the Pooh

472. A hero is born among a hundred, and they found a wise man among a thousand, but we might not find an accomplished one, even among a hundred thousand. — Plato

473. If human beings are perceived as potentials rather than problems, as possessing strength instead of weaknesses, as unlimited rather than dull and unresponsive, then they thrive and grow to their capabilities. — Barbara Bush

474. The flower doesn't dream of the bee. It blossoms and the bee comes. — Mark Ne

Chapter Six

Life Philosophy, Beliefs, Faith, Hope, and Love

In the Introduction above, the question was "What motivates you?" In this chapter, the question goes a little deeper: What do you live for? What do you value the most? Is there a greater purpose that drives you, day-by-day?

These wisdom keys and quotes range from Buddha to the New Testament, representing core beliefs that some individuals not only find inspirational, but also find absolutely necessary to shape and guide their lives in all aspects. These beliefs go beyond "feel good" sayings or tried-and-true aphorisms. Perhaps you see life, work, meaning, and relationships in a different light, but you'll find some profound statements and tenets here that have driven countless individuals to achieve their goals, improve their lives, and mark their legacies for the future. These quotations encompass what we believe, feel, and hope within ourselves, as well as what we believe, feel, hope, and seek outside ourselves.

~ ~ ~ ~

475. People inspire you or they drain you. Pick them wisely. — Hans F. Hasen

476. Your future needs you. Your past doesn't. — Anonymous

477. One day the people that don't even believe in you will tell everyone how they met you. — Johnny Depp

478. Focus on your true purpose of life and stop focusing on other people's flaws, mistakes, and failures. The fulfillment of your positive purpose on earth truly needs your undivided attention. — Edmond Mbiaka

479. Be very careful, then, how you live — not as unwise but as wise, making the most of every opportunity, because the days are evil. — The Bible, Ephesians 5:16-16

480. Stop waiting for the right time. Time isn't waiting for you. — Unknown

481. I never lose. I either win or I learn. — Nelson Mandela

482. If you believe it will work out you'll see opportunities. If you believe it won't, you will see obstacles. — Wayne Dyer

483. Fall seven times, stand up eight. — Japanese proverb

484. What always seems miraculous is when aesthetic necessities yield an insight which otherwise I would have missed. — Susan Griffin

485. The best things are yet to come. Trust yourself. — Unknown

486. A calm mind makes a wiser decision. Patience is power. — Unknown

487. If you can't figure out your purpose, figure out your passion. For your passion will lead you right into your purpose. — Bishop T. D. Jakes

488. Singleness of purpose is one of the chief essentials for success in life, no matter what may be one's aim. — John D. Rockefeller

489. The soul which has no fixed purpose in life is lost; to be everywhere, is to be nowhere. — Nichel de Montaigne

490. When you find your "why", you don't hit the snooze no more! You find a way to make it happen. — Eric Thomas

491. The person without a purpose is like a ship without a rudder. — Thomas Carlyle

492. Figure out what your purpose is in life, what you really and truly want to do with your time and your life, then be willing to sacrifice everything and then some to achieve it. If you are not willing to make the sacrifice, then keep searching. — Quintina Ragnacci

493. Life becomes easier when you learn to accept an apology you never got. — Robert Brault

494. May your choices reflect your hopes, not your fears. — Nelson Mandela

495. Let the beauty of what you love be what you do. — Rumi

496. The time is always right to do what is right. — Martin Luther King, Jr.

497. Not all who wander are lost. — J. R. R. Tolkien

498. You may say I'm a dreamer, but I'm not the only one. I hope someday you'll join us. And the world will live as one. —John Lennon

499. You must be the change you wish to see in the world. — Mahatma Gandhi

500. Spread love everywhere you go. Let no one ever come to you without leaving happier. —Mother Teresa

501. The only thing we have to fear is fear itself. — Franklin D. Roosevelt

502. Darkness cannot drive out darkness: only light can do that. Hate cannot drive out hate: only love can do that. —Martin Luther King Jr.

503. In the depths of winter, I finally learned that within me there lay an invincible summer. — Albert Camus

504. I alone cannot change the world, but I can cast a stone across the water to create many ripples. — Mother Teresa

505. You become what you believe. — Oprah Winfrey

506. All our experience with history should teach us, when we look back, how badly human wisdom is betrayed when it relies on itself. — Martin Luther

507. It's worth remembering that the greatest gain in terms of wisdom and inner strength is often that of greatest difficulty. — Dalai Lama

508. It is undoubtedly easier to believe in absolution, follow blindly, mouth received wisdom. But that is self-betrayal. — John Ralston Saul

509. A mother is clothes with strength and dignity, laughs without fear of the future. When she speaks, her words are wise and she gives instructions with kindness. — Proverbs 31:25

510. The ignorant work for their own profit; the wise work for the welfare of the world, without thought for themselves. — *Bhagavad Gita*

511. "What can I learn from this challenge? What is it teaching me?" Then he would stay positive and trust that the lessons would make him stronger, wiser, better. — Unknown

512. Drop by drop is the water pot filled. Likewise, the wise man, gathering it little by little fills himself with good. — The Buddha (Dhammapada)

513. To search for wisdom apart from Christ means not simply foolhardiness but utter insanity. — John Calvin

514. He how (tries to) govern a state by his wisdom is a scourge to it; while he who does not (try to) do so is a blessing. — Lao Tzu

515. Giving birth and being born brings us into the essence of creation, where the human spirit is courageous and bold and the body, a miracle of wisdom. — Harriette Hartigan

516. Whatever your hand finds to do, do it with your might; for there is no work or device or knowledge or wisdom in the grave where you are going. — Ecclesiastes 9:10

517. Knowing others is intelligence. Knowing yourself is true wisdom. Mastering others is strength. Mastering yourself is true power. — Lao Tzu

518. Win over an egoist by showing him respect, a wise person by truth, and a crazy person by letting him behave in an insane manner. — Chanakya

519. If a man devotes himself to art, much evil is avoided that happens otherwise if one is idle. — Albrecht Durer

520. History teaches us that men and nations behave wisely once they have exhausted all other alternatives. — Abba Eban

521. The money you are looking for is not in any country, PhD or your designer outlook, it is in wisdom. Solomon never prayed for wealth but he asked for wisdom. — Patience Johnson

522. If we could renounce our sageness and discard our wisdom, it would be better for the people a hundredfold. — Lao Tzu

523. God, grant me the serenity to accept the things I cannot change, the courage to change the things I can, and wisdom yo know the difference. — Reinhold Niebuhr

524. Where does a wise man kick a pebble? On the beach. Where does a wise man hide a leaf? In the forest. — G. K. Chesterton

525. It is worth remembering that the time of greatest gain in terms of wisdom and inner strength is often that of greatest difficulty. — Dalai Lama

526. The wisdom of the Moon is greater than the wisdom of the Earth, because the Moon sees the universe better than the Earth can see it! — Mehmet Murat Idan

527. Of all the things which wisdom provides to make us entirely happy, much the greatest is the possession of friendship. — Epicurus

528. The level of your wisdom and unwavering faith in Christ is what I have always admired. Thanks for all you o in the church and for the church. — Unknown

529. When it comes to making friends, it is never about how many you have, but about the kind of energy that they bring. Please choose wisely. — Edmond Mbiaka

530. The wise man does not lay up his own treasures. The more he gives to others, the more he has for his own. — Lao Tzu

531. If I were rain/ That joins the sky and earth that otherwise never touch/ Could I join two hearts as well? — Tite Kubo

532. Wisdom ceases to be wisdom when it becomes too proud to weep, too grave to laugh, and too selfish to seek other than itself. — Kahlil Gibran

533. Through the portals of silence, the healing sun of wisdom and peace will shine upon you. — Paramahansa Yogananda

534. Sunset is always wiser than sunrise because sunset has added the experience of an entire day to his soul! — Mehmet Murat Ildan

535. None can destroy iron, but its own rust can! Likewise, no one can destroy us; but our own mindset can. — Ratan Tata

536. If you wish to get rich, save what you get. A fool can earn money, but it takes a wise man to save and dispose of it to his own advantage. — Brigham Young

537. If we aren't walking in wisdom, intimacy, and understanding with our Lord, we are walking in folly. And folly's ways lead to death. —Unknown

538. If a purple tulip could talk she would say something calm, cool and wise, without the flash of a soothing balm. — Amelia Brown, *A Poem of Encouragement*

539. If you keep your heart open through everything, your pain can become your greatest ally in your life's search for love and wisdom. — Rumi

540. Through the portals of silence, the healing sun of wisdom and peace will shing upon you. — Paramahansa Yogananda

541. The teacher who is indeed wise does not bid you to enter the house of his wisdom, but rather leas you to the threshold of your mind. — Kahlil Gibran

542. The guiding factor in a decision is often not the one that counsels most wisely; it's one that has recently been brought to mind. — Cialdini

543. I would go out into the desert. The desert was my teacher. I didn't know about gurus and wise people. I wasn't a reader. — Byron Katie

544. Wise women tuck Godly wisdom into the words they speak and even more into the words they choose not to speak. — Lysa TerKeurst

545. This storm will pass. Although, it has tested our strength, our foundations, our roots, we will arise stronger, wiser, and smarter. The best is yet to come. — Charles F. Glassman

546. Our own worst enemy cannot harm us as much as our unwise thought. No one can help us as much as our own compassionate thoughts. — Buddha

547. The secret of health for both mind and body is not to mourn for the past, nor to worry about the

548. future, but to live the present moment wisely and earnestly. — Yesenia Chavan

549. The field of the soul must be watered by the rain with tears of love; otherwise, it will become a desert. — Sorin Cerin

550. Hardships often prepare ordinary people for an extraordinary destiny. — C. S. Lewis

551. We are able to feel and learn very quickly through music, through art, through poetry, some special things that we would otherwise learn very slowly. — Boyd K. Packer

552. Withhold a smile only when the smile can hurt someone. Otherwise, let it bloom forth in a riot. — Vera Nazarian

553. What is stronger than the human heart which shatters over and over and still lives? — Rupi Kaur

554. Pain makes you stronger. Tears make you braver. Heartbreak makes you wiser. And vodka makes you not remember any of that crap. — Nishan Panwar

555. He who puts his brother in the ground is everywhere. The word of the wise has fled without delay. Lo, the son of man is denied recognition. — Possibly Matthew 7:24

556. Hope is sweet. Hope is illuminating. Hope is fulfilling. Hope can be everlasting. Therefore, do not give up hope, even in the sunset of your life. — Sri Chinmoy

557. Man is nothing else but what he makes of himself. — John-Paul Sartre

558. Your core beliefs are the deeply held beliefs that authentically describe your soul. — John Maxwell

559. Man are not disturbed by events, but by the views to which they take them. — Epictus

560. To say goodbye is to die a little. — Raymond Chandler, *The Long Goodbye*

561. The first and greatest victory is to conquer yourself. — Plato

562. What you think, you become. — Buddha

563. Don't let the perfect be the enemy of the good. — Voltaire

564. Everything we hear is an opinion, not a fact. Everything we see is a perspective, not the truth. — Marcus Aurelius

565. We don't see things as they are, we see them as we are. — Anais Nin

566. The single-story creates stereotype, and the problem with stereotypes is not that they are untrue, but that they are incomplete. They make one story become the only story. — Chimamanda Ngozi Adichie

567. Your path is at your feet whether you realize it or not. — Agnes Martin

568. The weak can never forgive. Forgiveness is the attribute of the strong. — Mahatma Gandhi

569. Legging go gives us freedom, and freedom is the only condition for happiness. If, in our heart, we will cling to anything — anger, anxiety, or possessions — we cannot be free. — Thich Nhat Hanh

570. In their seeking, wisdom and madness are one and the same. On the path of love, friend and stranger are one and the same. — Rumi

571. God is too good to be unkind. He is too wise to be confused. If I cannot trace His hand, I can always trust His heart. — Charles Spurgeon Unknown

572. If any of you lacks wisdom, you should ask God, who gives generously to all without finding fault, and it will be given to you. — James 1:5

573. Lord, help us to see trouble coming long before it gets here. And give us the wisdom to know what to do and the courage to do it. — Anonymous

574. Observe the life by cause and consequence. Explore the life by wisdom. Treat the life by equality. Complete the life by love. — Guatama Buddha

575. The beginning of love is to let those we love be perfectly themselves, and not to twist them to fit our own image. Otherwise, we love only the reflection of ourselves we see. — Thomas Merton

576. Meditation rings wisdom; lack of meditation leaves ignorance. Know well what leads you forward and what holds you back and choose the path that leads to wisdom. — Buddha

577. Let me tell you what mature people do. They get stronger. They get wiser, They get better. Not a bad idea, to use the winter for personal development. — Unknown

578. If a rich man ate a snake, they would say it was because of his wisdom. If a poor man ate it, they would say it was because of his stupidity. — Lebanese proverb

579. Your soul is the power and core of who you are. Feed it well. — Anonymous

580. Two axes in a basket will always clash. — African proverb

581. Great is many, many individual feats, and each of them is doable. — Dan Chamblis

582. Discovering more joy dos not, I'm sorry to say, save us from the inevitability of hardships and heartbreaks. Yet as we discover more joy, we can face suffering in a way that ennobles rather than embitters. We have hardship without becoming hard. We have heartbreak without being broken. — Desmond Tutu

583. Grief is the price we pay for love. — Queen Elizabeth II, speaking about September 11, 2001

584. Hope is the active conviction that despair will never have the last word. — Cory Booker

~ ~ ~ ~

Tyler Perry quotes:

585. It doesn't matter if a million people tell you what you can't do, or if ten million tell you no. If you get one yes from God that's all you need. — Tyler Perry

586. The Bible says that all things work together for the good of those who love the Lord and are called according to his purpose. I believe that. Because I've seen it all work. — Tyler Perry

587. It takes a week to do a sitcom in Hollywood. I do a show a day in my studio, three or four shows a week. — Tyler Perry

588. I thank God I didn't become successful until I was older. — Tyler Perry

589. If you don't want my God here, you don't want me here either. God has been too good to me to go and try to sell out to get some money. — Tyler Perry

590. My biggest success is getting over the things that have tried to destroy and take me out of this life. Those are my biggest successes. It has nothing to do with work. — Tyler Perry

591. It's not an easy journey, to get to a place where you forgive people. But it is such a powerful place because it frees you. — Tyler Perry

592. My mother was truly my saving grace, because she would take me to church with her. I would see my mother smiling in the choir, and I wanted to know this God that made her so happy. If I had not had that faith in my life, I don't know where I would be right now. — Tyler Perry

593. Happiness for me is totally just being at peace knowing that, everything I'm doing, God is pleased with that. It's complete peace for me. — Tyler Perry

594. You know what the question is that a lot of people ask me all the time, 'How did you make it, how did you make it?' Well I tell you there is only one answer for that,…..The truth be told, it was nothing but the grace of God…..I say this in the press all the time but people will cut it out of articles or they don't want to print it or they don't want to say it. — Tyler Perry

595. I've never chased money. It's always been about what I can do to motivate and inspire people. — Tyler Perry

596. You can't build your life around hurts from the past. — Tyler Perry

597. I'm not afraid to have a character say, 'I am a Christian,' or, 'I believe in God,' because I think they represent real people on this Earth. — Tyler Perry

598. I'm not sure why no one wants to admit there's a viable audience out there that believes in God and wants to see a movie with their family. The demand is there. The supply is not. — Tyler Perry

599. All you can do is plant your seed in the ground, water it and believe. — Tyler Perry

600. Don't believe the hype. I don't care how many number ones you have at the box office; I don't care how much they say you're great, don't believe it. Just stay in your lane and do what you're supposed to do. — Tyler Perry

601. You can never be upset with the people who forced you into your dream or up higher. — Tyler Perry

602. I didn't have a catharsis for my childhood pain, most of us don't, and until I learned how to forgive those people and let it go, I was unhappy. — Tyler Perry

~ ~ ~ ~

Chapter Seven

Wisdom: A Wise Life Well-Lived

"Wisdom" has been a recurring theme here, but how we define or recognize it varies with circumstances, our perspectives on life, work, success and well being. These quotes reflect the inter-relationships among living, working, success, failure, forgiveness, and feelings. A life well-lived is portrayed here as one in which there is both balance and space: There is balance among all aspects of our lives, and there is always space for improvement, reflection, growth, goal-setting, and success.

When we are wise, we are able to see things more clearly than when our vision is clouded by fatigue, confusion, or feeling overwhelmed. When we are wise, we can take risks, reach out to others, and take better care of ourselves and our loved ones. When we are wise, we are humble enough to know, as Mother Teresa stated above, that we are capable of making small changes that produce ripples that reach into the world.

Wisdom is often associated with age, as if those who are older just absorb wisdom with each passing year. A life well-lived is often associated with wealth, power, possessions, and the power to set trends and influence the lives of others. You may find, though, that there are many more layers and nuances to both wisdom and a well-lived life. Why? Because, at the core of it, wisdom requires continual learning, adapting, growing, and even recovering from failure.

~ ~ ~ ~

603. Happiness is not a goal. It's a by-product of a life well-lived. — Eleanor Roosevelt

604. Don't be so bitter about a bad experience from your past that you miss the opportunities in front of you. — Robert Kiyosaki

605. You are closer than you think. — Unknown

606. No one is actually dead until all the ripples they cause in the world die away. — Terry Pratchett

607. There is only one proof of ability — action. — Marie von Ebner- Eschenbach

608. Normality is a paved road. It's comfortable to walk, but no flowers grow on it. — Vincent van Gogh

609. The past is a place of reference, not a place of residence; the past is a place of learning, not a place of living. — Roy T. Bennett

610. You only pass through life once; you don't come back for an encore. — Elvis Presley

611. Growth demands a temporary surrender of security. It may mean giving up familiar but limiting patterns, safe but unrewarding work, values no longer believed in, and relationships that have lost their meaning. — John C. Maxwell

612. Freedom is never given; it is won. — A. Philip Randolph

613. I can't change the direction of the wind, but I can adjust my sails to always reach my destination. — Jimmy Dean

614. If you don't try, nothing will ever happen. — Unknown

615. The successful warrior is the average man, with laser-like focus. — Bruce Lee

616. Perfection is not attainable, but if we chase perfection we can catch excellence. — Vince Lombardi

617. Be proud. You survived the days you thought you couldn't. —Unknown

618. Adventure should be 80 percent, "I think this is manageable," but it's good to have that last 20 percent where you're right outside your comfort zone. Still safe, but outside your comfort zone. — Bear Grylls

619. Big dreams require healthy habits and healthy habits require self-discipline. —Unknown

620. Breathe. It's only a bad day, not a bad life. — Johnny Depp

621. Stop calling it a dream and start calling it a plan. —The Purpose Exchange

622. Remain focused. Your time is coming. — Unknown

623. Be brutally honest about the short term and optimistic and confident about the long term. — Reed Hastings

624. Win in your mind and you will win in your reality. — The Mindset Journey

625. Confidence is built by facing what you fear. — Christina Gardner

626. Don't complain, rebuild yourself. — *Attitude Move*

627. Never let your emotions overpower your intelligence. — Drake

628. The world belongs to the enthusiast who keeps cool. — William McFee

629. The greatest glory in living lies not in falling, but in rising every time we fall. — Nelson Mandela

630. You can't cross the sea merely by standing and staring at the water. — Rabindranath Tagore

631. Look forward with hope, not backward with regret. — Unknown

632. The only safe thing to do is to take a chance. — Elaine May

633. Your world is a living expression of how you are using and have used your mind. — Earl Nightingale

634. Nobody is coming to save you. Get up and be your own hero. —Kevin Mangelschots

635. The quality of your thinking determines the quality of your life. — A. R. Bernard

636. Become a ghost. Forget attention. Just grow in private. — Jake Frosher

637. Your world is a living expression of how you are using and have used your mind. — Earl Nightingale

638. Nobody is coming to save you. Get up and be your own hero. —Kevin Mangelschots

639. The quality of your thinking determines the quality of your life. — A. R. Bernard

640. The price of greatness is responsibility. — Winston Churchill

641. Whatever the present moment contains, accept it as if you had chosen it. — Eckhart Tolle

642. Don't overshare. Privacy is power. — Lewin, *Wealth Pill*

643. Never tolerate disrespect, not even from yourself. —Charles Sledge

644. Keep it private until it's permanent. — *Divine Manhood*

645. Two things define you: Your patience when you have nothing and your attitude when you have everything. — Unknown

646. If you see someone without a smile, give 'em yours. — Dolly Parton

647. Value your peace of mind. — Unknown

648. Attention is the rarest and purest form of generosity. — Simone Weil

649. Take the risk or lose the chance. — Unknown

650. We lose ourselves in things we love. We find ourselves there, too. — Kristin Martz

651. In art, as in love, instinct is enough. — Anatole France

652. Give a man a fish and you feed him for a day. Teach a man to fish, feed him for a lifetime.— Unknown

653. Die with memories, not dreams. — Anonymous

654. Everything you can imagine is real. — Pablo Picasso

655. It's not enough to have lived. We should be determined to live for something. — Winston Churchill

656. The mystery of human existence lies not in just staying alive, but in finding something to live for. — Fyodor Dostoyevsky

657. Don't you know your imperfections are a blessing? Kendrick Lamar

658. Dogs are wise. They crawl away into a quiet corner and lick their wounds and do not rejoin the world until they are whole once more. — Agatha Christie

659. Great minds have purposes, others have wishes. — Washington Irving

660. The heart of human excellence often begins to beat when you discover a pursuit that absorbs you, frees you, challenges you, or gives you a sense of meaning, joy, or passion. — Terry Orlick

661. You were put on this earth to achieve your greatest self, to live out your purpose, and to do it courageously. — Steve Maraboli, *Life, the Truth, and Being Free*

662. Determine your priorities and focus on them. — Unknown

663. Try to be a rainbow in someone's cloud. — Maya Angelou

664. Believe in yourself, take on your challenges, dig deep within yourself to conquer fear. Never let anyone bring you down. You got to keep going. — Chantal Sutherland

665. What am I living for and what am I dying for are the same question. — Margaret Atwood

666. If you can tune into your purpose and really align with it, setting goals so that your vision is an expression of that purpose, then life flows much more easily. — Jack Canfield

667. If the whole world was blind, how many people would you impress? — Boonaa Mohammed

668. Life is like riding a bicycle. To keep your balance, you must keep moving. — Albert Einstein

669. Life is not a problem to be solved, but a reality to be experienced. — Soren Kierkegaard

670. The big lesson in life, baby, is never be scared of anyone or anything. — Frank Sinatra

671. Too many of us are not living our dreams because we are living our fears. — Les Brown

672. Life is about making an impact not, making an income. — Kevin Kruse, *Forbes*

673. The greatest pleasure of life is love. —Euripides

674. To improve is to change; to be perfect is to change often. — Winston Churchill

675. Today, you have 100% of your life left. — Tom Hopkins

676. You will face many defeats in life, but never let yourself be defeated. — Maya Angelou

677. It is during our darkest moments that we must focus to see the light. — Aristotle

678. If life were predictable, it would cease to be life and be without flavor. — Eleanor Roosevelt

679. Positive anything is better than negative nothing. — Elbert Hubbard

680. Life is a succession of lessons which must be lived to be understood. — Ralph Waldo Emerson

681. Try not to become a man of success, rather become a man of value. — Albert Einstein

682. Every accomplishment begins with the decision to try. — John F. Kennedy

683. You have brains in your head. You have feet in your shoes. You can steer yourself any direction you choose. — Dr. Seuss

684. Life is either a daring adventure or nothing. — Helen Keller

685. Winning isn't everything, but wanting to win is. — Vince Lombardi

686. I've learned over the years that when one's mind is made up, this diminishes fear. — Rosa Parks

687. Twenty years from now you will be more disappointed by the things that you didn't do than by the ones you did do. So, throw off the bowlines, sail away from safe harbor, catch the trade winds in your sails. Explore. Dream. Discover. — Mark Twain

688. When wisdom comes, transformation comes. Wisdom makes the difference between the succeeding man and the failing man. — Patience Johnson

689. Sometimes the subconscious mind manifests a wisdom several steps or even years ahead of the conscious mind and has its own way of leading us towards our destiny. — Nathaniel Brandon

690. The beginning of wisdom is knowing which way is the high road and going through it. The view is always better from the high road. Don't deny yourself the beautiful view. — Anonymous

691. Great difficulties may be surmounted by patience and perseverance. — Abigail Adams

692. Comedy is acting out optimism. — Robin Williams

693. Nostalgia, more than anything, gives us the shudder of our own imperfection. — Emil Cloran

694. The main thing is not to hurry. Nothing good gets away. — John Steinbeck

Chapter Eight

Work, Work, Work

A quick search for "motivational quotes about work" yielded 3.8 million results. If "work" is paired with other words like "success," or "home," the results increase. If you pair "work," "inspirational" and "encouraging" the selection is even bigger.

The concept of "work" has changed dramatically in the last three years, most notably in the expansion of "work at home" or "remote work" opportunities. Workers who formerly had to navigate traffic, road construction, and over-crowded parking areas now merely must navigate their way to the kitchen table, the home office desk, or the most comfortable chair in the den. At a different tier, workers who make minimum wage are still challenged to make ends meet, sometimes through working multiple jobs.

We all know what work is because we all do it, whether we receive a salary or other compensation or not. There are thousands — perhaps millions — of women and men who are "stay-at-home" parents; arguably, they work harder and longer hours than anyone who clocks in at 9AM and out at 5PM, then leaves their office.

Clearly, the option of working at home came close on the heels of having to school our children at home because of the pandemic. Of course, that new arrangement deeply affected the day care industry, teachers, administrators and other school staff, bus drivers, cabbies, and other independent drivers. At the same time, there appeared to be a boom in home deliveries of anything one might imagine, so stores and local businesses that employed us, our loved ones, or our neighbors suffered from that negative impact.

Thes quotes about work are varied. In fact, you've already read some related quotes that could have been in this chapter but worked as well, if not better, in previous chapters. For example, in the first chapter, one anonymous motivational quote stated: "To be the best, you must be able to handle the worst." While that is a very good idea in general, it has come into play in these last years when "being the best" at work not only meant "handling the worst," but also meant working in the kitchen while the children are learning math beside you, your spouse is down with the flu, and the new puppy has discovered shoes are wicked-good chewy toys!

~ ~ ~ ~

695. They ask what I often refer to as the best question ever: "In light of my past experience, and my future hopes and dreams, what's the wise thing to do?" — John Stuart Mill

696. Six essential qualities that are the key to success: Sincerity, personal integrity, humility, courtesy, wisdom, charity. — Dr. William Menninger

697. You have to be pretty driven to make it happen. Otherwise, you will just make yourself miserable. — Elon Musk

698. Power is not what we do, but what we do not — hasty and unwise actions that we repeat every day and which ultimately bring us into trouble. — Robert Grene, *Mastery*

699. The intelligent investor will remember the wise words of financial analyst Mark Schweber: "Toe one question never to ask a bureaucrat is, 'Why?'" — Benjamin Graham

700. There is a problem with wise people. They always know what is wrong. So I never employ an expert in full bloom. — Henry Ford

701. The courage to imagine the otherwise is our greatest resource, adding color and suspense to all our life. — Daniel J. Boorstin

702. If you get up in the morning and think the future is going to be better, it is a bright day. Otherwise, it's not. — Elon Musk

703. We have to innovate for a specific reason, and that reason comes from the market. Otherwise, we'll end up making museum pieces. — Phil Knight

704. One, remember to look up at the stars and not down at your feet. Two, never give up work. Work gives you meaning and purpose, and life is empty without it. Three, if you are lucky enough to find love, remember it is there and don't throw it away. — Stephen Hawking

705. It's very important to like the people you work with, otherwise life [and] your job is gonna be quite miserable. — Elon Musk

706. Keep your head up. Be strong and take whatever hits you and make the best of it. Work hard, think wisely, and you will succeed. — Unknown

707. Sometimes it's not the money in your bank account that solves your problem, but the wisdom in your head. — Michael Bassey Johnson

708. All growth depends upon activity. There is no development physically or intellectually without effort, and effort means work. —Calvin Coolidge

709. Adding a deadline and incorporating one or multiple forms of urgency will get more people to take action than would otherwise. — LinkedIn

710. Be thankful for every new challenge. Each will give you more strength. wisdom and character. — Kristen Butler

711. Don't ask yourself what the world needs; ask yourself what makes you come alive. And then go and do that. Because what the world needs is people who have come alive. — Howard Thurman

712. If you think your boss is stupid, remember you wouldn't have a job if he was any smarter. — John Gotti

713. Five percent of the people think; ten percent of the people think they think; and the other eighty-five percent would rather die than think. — Thomas Edison

714. Even if it's been a while, you should remember your comrades' faces. Why? Because otherwise you will hurt their feelings when they call out to you. — Shino Aburame

715. If you bring a bunch of wolves into your circle, you better be damn sure to feed them. Otherwise, it won't be long before the pack turns on you. — Curtis Jackson, *Hustle Harader, Hustle Smarter*

716. Fishing is a hard job. Fishing at night. Rain, day, night…you have to be wise and smart. And quick. — Mariano Rivera

717. In politics, you learn how to say A but mean to say B. In wisdom you learn how to say A and keep saying that. — Auliq Ice

718. People's beliefs about their abilities have a profound effect on those abilities. Ability is not a fixed property. — Albert Bandura

719. Talent is just pursued interest. — Bob Ross

720. Love and work are the cornerstones of our maturity, of our humanness. — Sigmund Freud

721. Positive thinking will let you do everything better then negative thinking will. — Zig Ziglar

722. Growth demands a temporary surrender of security. It may mean giving up familiar but limiting patterns, safe but unrewarding work, values no longer believed in, and relationships that have lost their meaning. — John C. Maxwell

723. Obstacles don't have to stop you. If you run into a wall, don't turn around and give up. Figure out how to climb it, go through it, or work around it. — Michael Jordan

724. If your heart is attached to it, then your mind will be attached to it. — Vera Wang

725. There are two things to aim at in life: first, to get what you want, and after that, to enjoy it. Only the wisest of mankind achieve the second. — Logan Pearsall Smith

726. You cannot buy or win happiness; you must choose it. Like any discipline, your attitude will not take care of itself. You need to attend to it daily. — John Maxwell

727. Vision will get you inspired. Discipline will take you there. —Christine Caine

728. Don't rush the process, good things take time. —Lao Tzu

729. Change might not be fast and it isn't always easy. But with time and effort, almost any habit can be reshaped. — Charles Duhigg

730. If one morning I walked on top of the water across the Potomac River, the headline that afternoon would read: "President Can't Swim." — Lyndon B. Johnson

731. Champions don't do extraordinary things. They do ordinary things, but they do them without thinking, too fast for the other team to react. They follow the habits they've learned. —Charles Duhigg

732. Someone once defined hard work as the accumulation of the easy things you didn't do when you should have. — John Maxwell

733. We won't be distracted by comparison if we're captivated by purpose. — Bob Goff

734. A lot of fellows nowadays have a B. A., M. D., or Ph. D. Unfortunately, they don't have a J. O. B. — Fats Domino

735. You may have a million reasons not to get started now. But deep down, none of them can be as compelling as your desire to change, grow, and succeed. In a month or a year or five years from now, you may have only one regret — that you didn't start now. Today matters. The way you spend today really can change your life. — John Maxwell

736. Let's stop the glorification of busy. We don't need to use our busyness as a measure of worthiness — Jennifer Pastiloff.

737. People often say motivation doesn't last, well, neither does bathing- that's why we recommend it daily — Zig Ziglar.

738. To do anything really well, you have to overextend yourself .in doing something over and over again, something that was never natural becomes second to nature.... The capacity to do something diligently doesn't come overnight. — John Irving

739. Passion for your work is a little bit about discovery, followed by development, and then a lifetime of deepening. —Angela Duckworth

740. Don't let the perfect be the enemy of the good. —Voltaire

741.......the most important thing you could do, is to do a lot of work. Do a huge volume of work. — Ira Glass

742. You call it procrastination; I call it thinking. — Adam Grant

743. There need to be reasons to get up in the morning. Life can't just be about solving problems, otherwise, what's the point? — Elon Musk

744. Procrastination is a self-defeating behavior pattern marker by short term benefits and long-term costs. — Roy Baumeister

745. Fear is the darkroom where negatives are developed. —Michael Pritchard

746. Fear is when I have caution over a real and present danger. Anxiety is when I have caution over a future imagined danger. — Myron Golden.

747. You can choose courage, or you can choose comfort, but you cannot choose both. —Brené Brown

748. Courage is not the absence of fear, but rather the judgment that something else is more important than one's fear. —Ambrose Redmoon

749. Confidence is silent. Insecurities are loud. Remember that. — Unknown

750. If we only wanted to be happy, it would be easy; but we want to be happier than other people, which is almost always difficult since we think them happier than they are. —Charles de Montesquieu

751. Formal education will make you a living; self-education will make you a fortune. —Jim Rohn

752. Self-education is, I firmly believe, the only kind of education there is. —Isaac Asimov

753. Wisdom is not a product of schooling but of the lifelong attempt to acquire it. —Albert Einstein

754. Our emotions need to be as educated as our intellect. It is important to know how to feel, how to respond, and how to let life in so that it can touch you. —Jim Rohn

755. Don't sweat the small stuff…….and it's all small stuff. —Richard Carlson

756. You will never reach your destination if you stop and throw stones at every dog that barks. —Winston Churchill

757. Comparison is the thief of joy. —Theodore Roosevelt

758. Possessing a great attitude is like having a secret weapon. —John Maxwell, *Today Matters*

759. You can control two things: your work ethic and your attitude about anything. — Ali Krieger

760. The best entrepreneurs are not risk maximizers; they take the risk out of risk-taking. — Linda Rottenberg

761. Many entrepreneurs take plenty of risks, but those are generally the failed entrepreneurs, not the success stories. —Malcolm Gladwell.

762. Eighty-percent of success is showing up. — Woody Allen

763. Devoting a little of yourself to everything means committing a great deal of yourself to nothing. —Michael Leboef

764. Never give up on a dream because of the time it will take to accomplish it. The time will pass anyway. —Earl Nightingale

765. The art of being wise is the art of knowing what to overlook. — William James

766. The only thing that ever sat its way to success was a hen. — Sarah Brown

767. Cows run away from the storm while the buffalo charges toward it — and gets through it quicker. Whenever I am confronted with a tough challenge, I do not prolong the torment, I become the buffalo. — Wilma Mankiller

768. The moment when you want to quit is the moment when you need to keep pushing. — Paulo Coelho

769. If you can't explain it simply, you don't understand it well enough. — Albert Einstein

770. The difference between winning and losing is most often not quitting. — Walt Disney

771. The worst enemy to creativity is self-doubt. — Sylvia Plath

772. Anyone who stops learning is old, whether at twenty or eighty. Anyone who keeps learning stays young. — Henry Ford

773. Don't compare yourself with anyone in the world…if you do so, you are insulting yourself. — Bill Gates

774. Someone is sitting in the shade today because someone planted a tree a long time ago. — Warren Buffet

775. All your life, you were only waiting for this moment to arrive. — *Blackbird*, the Beatles 1968

776. The man who can drive himself further, once the effort gets painful, is the man who will win. — Rober Bannister

777. Opportunity is missed by most people because it is dressed in overalls and looks like work. — Thomas Edison

778. The important thing is not to stop questioning. Curiosity has its own reason for existence. — Albert Einstein

779. We may encounter many defeats but we must not be defeated. — Maya Angelou

780. One day in retrospect the years of struggle will strike you as the most beautiful. — Sigmund Freud

781. We need to accept that we won't always make the right decisions, that we'll screw up royally sometimes — understanding that failure is not the opposite of success, it's part of success. — Arianna Huffington

782. Opportunity is missed by most people because it is dressed in overalls and looks like work. — Thomas Edison

783. A rockpile ceases to be a rock pile the moment a single man contemplates it, bearing within him the image of a cathedral. — Antoine de Saint-Exuprey

784. There is no substitute for hard work. — James J. Hill

785. Problems are not stop signs; they are guidelines. — Robert H. Schuller

786. The expectations of life depend upon diligence; the mechanic that would perfect his work must first sharpen his tools. — Confucius

787. Do what you have to do until you can do what you want. — Oprah Winfrey

788. If you organize your life around your passion, you can turn your passion into your story and then turn your story into something bigger — something that matters. — Blake Mycoskie

789. Chase your passion, not your pension. — Denis Waitley

790. This is why we likewise need positive messages for work that may help us persevere more to achieve our goals. — Unknown

791. Beware the soul-sucking force of "reasonableness." Otherwise you risk deflating your peaks. Speed bumps are reasonable. Mount Everest is not reasonable. — Chip and Dan Heath, *The Power of Moments*

792. The more that companies share this conventional wisdom about how they compete, the greater the competitive convergence among them. — *Harvard Business Review*

793. It is our choices that show what we truly are, far more than our abilities. —From *Harry Potter*

794. You buy a car for transport, not to live at the gas station. Likewise, you earn money to access essentials, not to live at the shopping mall. — Abhijit Naskar

795. The brain is a wonderful organ. It starts working the moment you get up in the morning and does not stop until you get into the office. — Robert Frost

~ ~ ~ ~

Leadership, Managing, Mentoring, Teaching

796. You have to be able to psychologically help your players, support-wise, be in touch with them, so I think managing people is very important. — Phil Jackson

797. Contrary to popular wisdom and behavior, conflict is not a bad thing for a team. In fact, the fear of conflict is almost always a sign of problems. — Patrick Lencioni

798. The skillful employer of men will employ the wise man, the brave man, the covetous man, and the stupid man. — Sun Tzu

799. Toxic positivity is pressuring people to look on the bright side…Healthy support is shielding people from the dark side. You invite them to express their pain, and show them they're not alone and won't feel it forever. — Adam Grant

800. I love deadlines. I love the whooshing noise they make as they go by. — Douglas Adams

801. It's a stupid leader who can't turn follower when somebody offers him a wiser course. — Orson Scott Card

802. A wise person grooms his child carefully, because only an educated person with high morale is given true respect in society. — Chanakya

803. The success of every woman should be the inspiration to another. We should raise each other up. Make sure you're very courageous. Be strong, be extremely kind, and above all, be humble. — Serena Williams

804. Women are the architects of society. — Harriet Beecher Stowe

805. The purpose of a politician is to be a leader. A politician has to lead. Otherwise he's just a follower. — Alan Greenspan

806. Effective leadership — and again this is very old wisdom — is not based on being clever; it is based primarily on being consistent. — Peter Drucker

807. Mentoring is a two-way street. The mentor gest wiser while mentoring, and the mentee gains knowledge through his/her mentor. — Marisol Gonzalez

808. I touch the future; I teach. — Christa McAuliffe

809. As we look ahead to the next century, leaders will be those who empower others. — Bill Gates

810. Speak to your children as if they are the wisest, kindest, most beautiful and magical humans on earth, for what they believe is what they will become. — Brooke Hampton

811. Being loyal to someone is a good thing…when it's reciprocated. Otherwise, you are only being their fool. — Unknown

812. Thus, what enables the wise sovereign and the good general to strike and conquer, and achieve things beyond the reach of ordinary men, is foreknowledge. — Sun Tzu

813. His wisdom for the ages said success lay in smiling, showing interest in other people, and making them feel good about themselves. — Leil Lowndes

814. As an older and wiser man, I don't believe in luck. I believe in hard work and talent and determination. — Dexter Fletcher

815. Power will intoxicate the best hearts, as wine the strongest heads. No man is wise enough, nor good enough to be trusted with unlimited power. — Charles Caleb Colton

816. One person might be senior and be wiser and have more experience, but I've learned a lot from the people I mentor. — Michelle Obama

817. Wise leaders generally have wise counselors because it takes a wise person themselves to distinguish them. — Diogenes

818. Too much leading and we create anxiety for children. Too much following and the same is true. In wisdom, we find balance between the two. — Vince Gowmon

819. Having a more experienced and successful counselor guiding someone in a chosen profession is a wise decision and good career move. — Jose A. Aviles

820. The way of a superior man is three-fold: Virtuous; he is free from anxieties; wise, he is free from perplexities, bold, he is free from fear. Confucius

821. Focus on talent distracts us from something that is at least as important, and that is effort. — Angela Duckworth

822. It is often the height of wisdom to find the perfect mentor and offer your services as an assistant for free. — Robert Greene, *Mastery*

823. Senior managers' goal here should be to manage their portfolio of business men to wisely balance between profitable growth and cash flow at a given point in time. — W. Chan Kim & Renee Mauborgne

824. Will people ever be wise enough to refuse to follow bad leaders or to take away the freedom of other people? — Eleanor Roosevelt

825. You cannot teach a man anything; you can only help him discover it in himself. — Galileo Galilei

826. There cannot be a stressful crisis this week. My schedule is already full. — Henry Kissinger

~ ~ ~ ~

Steve Jobs Quotes:

827. The only way to do great work is to love what you do. — Steve Jobs

828. Creativity is just connecting things. When you ask creative people how they did something, they feel a little guilty because they didn't really do it, they just saw something. It seemed obvious to them after a while. — Steve Jobs

829. It's really hard to design products by focus groups. A lot of times, people don't know what they want until you show it to them. —Steve Jobs

830. Remembering that you are going to die is the best way I know to avoid the trap of thinking you have something to lose. You are already naked. There is no reason not to follow your heart. — Steve Jobs

831. Be a yardstick of quality. Some people aren't used to an environment where excellence is expected. — Steve Jobs

832. You can't connect the dots looking forward; you can only connect them looking backward. So you have to trust that the dots will somehow connect in your future. You have to trust in something — your gut, destiny, life, karma, whatever. This approach has never let me down, and it has made all the difference in my life. — Steve Jobs

833. If you really look closely, most overnight successes took a long time. — Steve Jobs

834. Your work is going to fill a large part of your life, and the only way to be truly satisfied is to do what you believe is great work. And the only way to do great work is to love what you do. If you haven't found it yet, keep looking. Don't settle. As with all matters of the heart, you'll know when you find it. And, like any great relationship, it just gets better and better as the years roll on. So keep looking until you find it. Don't settle. — Steve Jobs

835. Being the richest man in the cemetery doesn't matter to me ... Going to bed at night saying we've done something wonderful ... that's what matters to me. — Steve Jobs

836. I'm as proud of many of the things we haven't done as the things we have done. Innovation is saying no to a thousand things. — Steve Jobs

837. I think if you do something and it turns out pretty good, then you should go do something else wonderful, not dwell on it for too long. Just figure out what's next. — Steve Jobs

838. Getting fired from Apple was the best thing that could have ever happened to me. The heaviness of being successful was replaced by the lightness of being a beginner again. It freed me to enter one of the most creative periods of my life. — Steve Jobs

839. Quality is more important than quantity. One home run is much better than two doubles. — Steve Jobs

840. When I was 17, I read a quote that went something like: "If you live each day as if it was your last, someday you'll most certainly be right." It made an impression on me, and since then, for the past 33 years, I have looked in the mirror every morning and asked myself: "If today were the last day of my life, would I want to do what I am about to do today?"

And whenever the answer has been 'no' for too many days in a row, I know I need to change something. — Steve Jobs

841. I'm convinced that about half of what separates successful entrepreneurs from the non-successful ones is pure perseverance. — Steve Jobs

842. I want to put a ding in the universe. — Steve Jobs

843. Your time is limited, so don't waste it living someone else's life. Don't be trapped by dogma — which is living with the results of other people's thinking. —Steve Jobs

844. It[what you choose to do] has got to be something that you're passionate about because otherwise you won't have the perseverance to see it through. —Steve Jobs

~ ~ ~ ~

Chapter Nine

Motivational Quotes and

Wisdom Keys Through the Ages

You've discovered quotes and keys for almost every aspect of your life, as well has quotes from individuals who have attained remarkable success, fame, achievement and, perhaps, notoriety...not to mention millions of dollars! Is one of them your role model? Do their lives reflect what you want your life to be? Maybe you see yourself as "the next" version of your role model, but people have been striving, succeeding, faltering, failing, and fortunate for centuries. Individuals and groups of people also have been handing down motivational sayings, adages, proverbs, and even humor since humans first joined one another to make the best of life. Warren Buffett has said, "Someone is sitting in the shade today because someone planted a tree a long time ago." That suggests we know that urging one another onward in the present will have an impact in the future.

Motivation, and the need for inspiration are universal, from the simple to the sublime. While we can compartmentalize inspirational quotes and wisdom keys into categories — as we've done here — it's also true that words of encouragement, criticism, envy and congratulations are timeless as well as applicable to all aspects of our lives. It would not be surprising in the least if each one of us has favorite sayings committed to memory. Maybe some of your favorite sayings are included here. From cheering on the hunters preparing to kill an animal large enough to feed the clan, to cheering when a $200,000,000,000 (yes, two-hundred billion) space shuttle ascends.

In their own words, here you'll find that what motivated Ancient Greeks, nomadic tribes, leaders of all kinds, and those who are creative. How do the words of Plato affect us today? The fact is that the sage words and lessons of Plato, Aristotle, Henry Ford, Albert Einstein, and Ruth Bader Ginsburg, and so many other "knowns" and "unknowns" still ring true today. Discover these statements, see some quotes that touch your mind, heart, soul, and life. Consider it a treasure hunt without a map.

Thousands of years of our human history has revealed we are not alone, we need one another, we are creative and innovative, and we learn from all our mistakes.

~ ~ ~ ~

845. Knowing yourself is the beginning of all wisdom. —Aristotle

846. The search for truth is more precious than its possession. — Gotthold Ephraim Lessing

847. The great use of life is to spend it for something that will outlast it. —William James

848. The purpose of life is to useful, to be honorable, to be compassionate, to have it make some difference that you have lived and lived well. — Ralph Waldo Emerson

849. Dare to be wise; begin! He who postpones the hour of living rightly is like the rustic who waits for the river to run out before he crosses. — Horace

850. Since we desire the true happiness that is brought about by a calm mind, and such peace of mind arises only from having a compassionate attitude, we need to make a concerted effort to develop compassion. — Dalai Lama

851. As a day well spent brings happy sleep, so a life well used brings happy death. — Leonardo da Vinci

852. Life is not measured by the number of breaths we take, but by the moments that take our breath away. — Maya Angelou

853. There are only two ways to life your life. One is as though nothing is a miracle The other is as though everything is a miracle. — Albert Einstein

854. In the end, it's not the years in your life that count, it's the life in your years. — Alfred Stieglitz

855. He who has a *why* to live can bear almost any *how* .— Friedrich Nietzsche

856. Don't go around saying the world owes you a living. The world owes you nothing. It was here first. — Mark Twain

857. All the art of living lies in a fine mingling of letting go and holding on. — Henry Ellis

858. A gem cannot be polished without friction, nor a man perfected without trials. — Seneca

859. The man is a success who has lived well, loved much, and laughed often. — Robert Louis Stevenson

860. Life becomes harder for us when we live for others, but it also becomes richer and happier. — Albert Schweitzer

861. You've got to get to the stage in life where going for it is more important than winning or losing. — Arthur Ashe

862. We live in a world requiring light and darkness…partnership and solitude sameness and difference…the familiar and the unknown. We love because it's the only true adventure. — Nikki Giovanni

863. As you know, life is an echo. We get what we give. — Zig Ziglar

864. A man's life is interesting primarily when he has failed, I will know. For it's a sign that he tried to surpass himself. — Georges Clemenceau

865. Letting go isn't about having the courage to release th past; it's about having the wisdom to embrace the present. — Steve Maraboli

866. Within you there is a stillness and a sanctuary to which you can retreat at any time. — Hermann Hesse

867. There is no such thing as a little freedom. Either you are all free or you are not free. — Walter Cronkite

868. The only limit to our realization of tomorrow will be our doubts of today. — Eleanor Roosevelt

869. Our potential is one thing; what we do with it is another. — Angela Duckworth

870. The way to get started is to quit talking and begin doing. — Walt Disney

871. Some people dream of success while others wake up and work. — Voltaire

872. Character cannot be developed in ease and quiet. Only through experience of trial and suffering can the soul be strengthened, ambition inspired, and success achieved. — Helen Keller

873. A journey of a thousand miles begins with a single step. — Chinese proverb

874. Growth is the only evidence of life. — John Henry Newman

875. Intellectual growth should commence at birth and cease only at death. — Albert Einstein

876. A beautiful thing is never perfect. — Egyptian proverb

877. The only person you are destined to become is the person you decide to be. — Ralph Waldo Emerson

878. You live but once; you might as well be amusing. — Coco Chanel

879. Love is not a vessel to be filled but a fire to be kindled. — Plutarch

880. Better times are coming; be patient. — Unknown

881. One day, in retrospect, the years of struggle will strike you as the most beautiful. — Sigmund Freud

882. Carry out a random act of kindness, with no expectation of reward, safe in the knowledge that one day someone might do the same for you. — Princess Diana

883. The beginning of love is not to let those we love be perfectly themselves, and not to twist them to fit our own image. Otherwise, we love only the reflections of ourselves we see. — Thomas Merton

884. The first and greatest victory is to conquer yourself. — Plato

885. Simplicity is the ultimate sophistication. — Leonardo da Vinci

886. Yesterday, you said tomorrow. Just do it. — Shia LaBeouf

887. Dream as if you'll live forever. Live as if you'll die today. — James Dean

888. Tough times never last but tough people do. — Robert H. Schuller

889. Happiness depends upon ourselves. — Aristotle

890. You can have anything you want — if you want it badly enough. You can be anything you want to be, do anything you set out to accomplish if you hold to that desire with singleness of purpose. — William Adams

891. To live is the rarest thing in the world. Most people just exist. — Oscar Wilde

892. Do not let your grand ambitions stand in the way of small but meaningful accomplishments. — Bryant H. McGill

893. True glory consists in doing what deserves to be written, in writing what deserves to be read, and in so living as to make the world happier and better for our living in it. — Pliny the Elder

894. Challenges are what make life interesting. Overcoming them is what makes life meaningful. — Joshua Marine

895. The purpose of life is to live it, to taste experience to the utmost, to reach out eagerly and without fear for newer and richer experience. — Eleanor Roosevelt

896. Lean forward into your life Begin each day as if it were on purpose. — Mary Anne Radmachernott

897. True happiness is not attained through self-gratification, but through fidelity to a worthy purpose. — Helen Keller

898. Not how long but how well you have lived is the main thing. — Lucius Annaeus Seneca

899. If you want to live a happy life, tie it to a goal, not to people or things. — Albert Einstein

900. If you can build a muscle, you can build a mindset. — Paul Corke

901. Your time is your most precious asset. Don't waste it. — Mel Robbins

902. The secret of success is constancy to purpose. — Benjamin Disraeli

903. Efforts and courage are not enough without purpose and direction. — John F. Kennedy

904. Happiness is within. It has nothing to do with how much applause you get or how many people praise you. Happiness comes when you believe that you have done something truly meaningful. — Martin Yan

905. Practice like you've never won. Perform like you've never lost. — Bernard F. Asuncion

906. Art hurts. Art urges voyages — and it is easier to stay home. — Gwendolyn Brooks

907. As you grow older, you will discover that you have two hands, one for helping yourself, the other for helping others. — Audrey Hepburn

908. Nothing is more honorable than a grateful heart. — Lucius Annaeus Seneca

909. In the end, some of your greatest pains become your greatest strengths. — Drew Barrymore

910. Do not dwell in the past, do not dream of the future, concentrate the mind on the present moment. — Gautama Buddha

911. Well done is better than well said. — Benjamin Franklin

912. Do not go where the path may lead, go instead where there is no path and leave a trail. — Ralph Waldo Emerson

913. Endure, put up with whatever comes you way; learn to overcome weakness and pain; push yourself to the breaking point, but never cave in, — Toni Nadal

914. Begin, be bold, and venture to be wise. — Horace

915. So we beat on, boats against the current, borne back ceaselessly into the past. — F. Scott Fitzgerald

916. Never let the fear of striking out keep you from playing the game. —Babe Ruth

917. Life is never fair, and perhaps it is a good thing for most of us that it is not. —Oscar Wilde

918. Don't worry when you are not recognized but strive to be worthy of recognition. —Abraham Lincoln

919. Life is really simple, but we insist on making it complicated. —Confucius

920. May you live all the days of your life. — Jonathan Swift

921. In the future, tell the truth and evaluate each one according to is work and accomplishments. The present is theirs the future, for which I have really worked, is mine — Nikola Tesla

922. Leave nothing for tomorrow that can be done today — Abraham Lincoln

923. Dreaming, after all, is a form of planning. — Gloria Steinem

924. But this journey is so much more than just that. It really is about learning to tell myself no and learning to make wiser choices. — Unknown

925. You will be wiser to form your own ideas of the value of your holdings, based on full reports from the company about its operations and financial position. —Warren Buffett

926. Life itself is the most wonderful fairy tale. —Hans Christian Andersen

927. Do not let making a living prevent you from making a life. —John Wooden

928. Go confidently in the direction of your dreams! Live the life you've imagined. —Henry David Thoreau

929. Keep smiling because life is a beautiful thing and there's so much to smile about. —Marilyn Monroe

930. The secret of success is to do the common thing uncommonly well. . —John D. Rockefeller, Jr.

931. The most difficult thing is the decision to act, the rest is merely tenacity. —Amelia Earhart

932. An unexamined life is not worth living. —Socrates

933. People who count their chickens before they are hatched act very wisely, because chickens run about so absurdly that is it quite impossible to count them accurately. . —Oscar Wilde

934. Everything you've ever wanted is on the other side of fear. —George Addair

935. Dream big and dare to fail. —Norman Vaughan

936. First, have a definite, clear practical ideal; a goal, an objective. Second, have the necessary means to achieve your ends, wisdom, money, materials, and methods. Third, adjust all your means to that end. —Aristotle

937. Courage is grace under pressure. —Ernest Hemingway

938. It is still best to be honest and truthful; to make the most of what we have; to be happy with simple pleasures; and have courage when things go wrong. —Laura Ingalls Wilder

939. Nothing is impossible, the word itself says, "I'm possible!" —Audrey Hepburn

940. It does not matter how slowly you go as long as you do not stop. —Confucius

941. Don't find fault, find a remedy: anyone can complain. —Henry Ford

942. A man may die, nations may rise and fall, but an idea lives on. —John F. Kennedy

943. A wise mother knows: It is her state of consciousness that matters. Her gentleness and clarity command respect. Her love creates security. — Vimala McClure

944. You never know what you can do until you have to do it. — Betty Ford

945. Faith grows when it is lived and shaped by love. — Pope Francis

946. We long to have again the vanished part, in spite of all its pain. — Sophocles

947. Mindfulness, also called wise attention, helps us see what we're adding to our experiences, not only during meditation but also elsewhere. — Sharon Salzberg

948. Between stimulus and response there is a space. In that space is our power to choose our response. In our response lies our growth and our freedom. — Viktor E. Frankl

949. I get by with a little help from my friends. — The Beatles, 1967

950. We can complain because rose bushes have thorns, or rejoice because thorn bushes have roses. — Abraham Lincoln

951. All work that is worth anything is done in faith. — Albert Schweitzer

952. Disappointment is the nurse of wisdom. — Sir Boyle Roche

953. Faith is not belief without proof, but [it is] trust without reservation. — D. Elton Trueblood

954. You will not complete your faith until you love one another. — Muhammad

955. We are always getting ready to live but never living. — Unknown

956. Of all things which wisdom provides to make us entirely happy, much the greatest is the possession of friendship. — Epicurus

957. Truth, like milk, arrives in the dark but even so, wise dogs don't bark. Only mongrels make it hard for the milkman to come [into] the yard. — Christopher Morley

958. Life will never, ever be easy. It will have moments and seasons of hard, but we can choose our hard, o let's choose wisely. — Unknown

959. Black women were created of brown sugar and warm honey, the sweetest thing to bless the earth. Be wary of anyone who tells you otherwise. — Alexandra Elle

960. A friend is like an owl, both beautiful and wise. Or perhaps a friend is like a ghost, whose spirit never dies. — Anonymous

961. The man of wisdom is never of two minds; the man of benevolence never worries; the man of courage is never afraid. — Confucius

962. Life is a daring adventure or nothing at all. — Helen Keller

963. Cultivate the habit of early rising. It is unwise to keep the head long on a level with the feet. — Henry David Thoreau

964. Within us is the soul of the whole, the wise silence, the universal beauty, the eternal One. — Ralph Waldo Emerson

965. Don't let anyone tell you otherwise. Not your grandma, not your dad, no one. And if you need to break things, then by God break them good and hard. — Patrick Ness

966. What a man is, he must be. — Abraham Maslow

967. Man's main task is to give birth to himself, to become what he potentially is. — Erich Fromm

968. In order to enjoy the good life, we need to be fully open to experience, live in the present moment, trust ourselves, take responsibility for our choices, and treat ourselves and others with unconditional positive regard. — Carl Rogers

969. Don't be too timid and squeamish about your actions. All life is an experiment. The more experiments you make, the better. — Ralph Waldo Emerson

970. The best years of your life are the ones in which you decide your problems are your own. You realize that you control your own destiny. — Albert Ellis

971. Everything's in the mind. That's where it all starts. Knowing what you want is the first step toward getting it. — Mae West

972. Discovering what you really want saves you endless confusion and wasted energy. Stuart Wilde

973. If you want to be happy, be. — Leo Tolstoy

974. To become what we ar, and to become what we can become, is the only end of life. — Robert Louis Stevenson

975. When you live in complete acceptance of what is, that is the end of all drama in your life. — Eckhart Tolle

976. Owning our story and loving ourselves through the process is the bravest thing we'll ever do. — Brene Brown

977. Improving our relationships is improving our mental health. —William Glasser

978. Don't let the perfect be the enemy of the good. — Voltaire

979. I can become quite angry and burning with anger, but I have never been bitter. Bitterness is a corrosive, terrible acid. It just eats you and makes you sick. — Maya Angelou

980. Forgiveness says you are given another chance to make a new beginning. — Desmond Tuto

981. When you know and respect your own inner nature, you know where you belong. — Benjamin Hoff

982. Nothing in life is to be feared, it is only to be understood. Now is the time to understand more, so that we may fear less. — Marie Curie

983. The visions we offer our children shape the future. It matters what those visions are. Often they become self-fulfilling prophecies. Dreams are maps. — Carl Sagan

984. Only put off until tomorrow what you are willing to die having left undone. — Pablo Picasso

985. The best and most beautiful things in the world cannot be seen or even touched — they must be felt with the heart. — Helen Keller

986. Better days are coming. Be patient. — Anonymous

987. Self-trust is the first secret of success. — Ralph Waldo Emerson

988. Don't quit. Nothing lasts forever, not even pain. — *Absolute Motivation*

989. When you live your life with an appreciation of coincidences and their meanings, you connect with the underlying field of infinite possibilities. — William James

990. The only real mistake is the one from which we learn nothing. — Henry Ford

991. Life was meant to be lived, and curiosity must be kept alive. One must never, for whatever reason, turn his back on life. — Eleanor Roosevelt

992. You cannot find peace by avoiding life. — Virginia Woolf

993. Grit is living life like it's a marathon, not a sprint. — Angela Duckworth

994. Don't wait for opportunity, create it. — G. B. Shaw

995. The way of a superior man is three-fold: virtuous, he is free from anxieties; wise, he is free from perplexities; bold, he is free from fear. — Confucius

996. No one shows a child the sky. — African proverb

997. To laugh often and much; to win the respect of intelligent

998. people and the affection of children; to earn the appreciation of honest critics and to endure the betrayal of false friends. To appreciate beauty; to find the best in others; to leave the world a bit better whether by a healthy child, a garden patch, or a redeemed social condition; to know that even one life has breathed easier because you have lived. This is to have succeeded. —Ralph Waldo Emerson

999. I am rather inclined to silence, and whether that be wise or not, it is at least more unusual nowadays to find a man who can hold his tongue than to find one who cannot. — Abraham Lincoln

1000. Discernment does not mean knowing the difference between what is right and what is wrong. Discernment means knowing the difference between what is right and what is nearly right. — Charles Spurgeon

About Kharis Publishing:

Kharis Publishing, an imprint of Kharis Media LLC, is a leading Christian and inspirational book publisher based in Aurora, Chicago metropolitan area, Illinois. Kharis' dual mission is to give voice to under-represented writers (including women and first-time authors) and equip orphans in developing countries with literacy tools. That is why, for each book sold, the publisher channels some of the proceeds into providing books and computers for orphanages in developing countries so that these kids may learn to read, dream, and grow. For a limited time, Kharis Publishing is accepting unsolicited queries for nonfiction (Christian, self-help, memoirs, business, health and wellness) from qualified leaders, professionals, pastors, and ministers.

Learn more at: https://kharispublishing.com/